MRAC

D0672048

THE BOOKSHOP BOOK

Also by Jen Campbell

non-fiction

Weird Things Customers Say in Bookshops
More Weird Things Customers Say in Bookshops

poetry

The Hungry Ghost Festival

THE BOOKSHOP BOOK

Jen Campbell

Constable • London

CONSTABLE

First published in Great Britain in 2014 by Constable

Copyright © Jen Campbell, 2014

7 9 10 8 6

The moral right of the author has been asserted.

All rights reserved.
No part of this publication may be reproduced, stored in a retrieval system,
or transmitted, in any form, or by any means, without the prior permission in
writing of the publisher, nor be otherwise circulated in any form of binding or cover
other than that in which it is published and without a similar condition including
this condition being imposed on the subsequent purchaser.

A CIP catalogue record for this book
is available from the British Library.

ISBN: 978-1-47211-666-6

Typesetting and design by Basement Press, Glaisdale
Printed and bound in Great Britain by CPI Group (UK) Ltd, Croydon CRO 4YY

Papers used by Constable are from well-managed forests
and other responsible sources

MIX
Paper from
responsible sources
FSC® C104740

Constable
an imprint of
Little, Brown Book Group
Carmelite House
5 Victoria Embankment
London EC4Y 0DZ

An Hachette UK Company
www.hachette.co.uk

www.littlebrown.co.uk

Open For The Strangest Adventures

This is a room of transpositions and tricks,
of tiny time machines lined up, a spectrum of spines.

In this room, two people kept apart
for three hundred pages can begin to love each other
at an altitude of fifteen hundred feet in the Sunday air.
And the air is turning, is it not? It is filling
with flesh smells and fruit smells,
it is thick with swarms of flitting black letters.

Life appears where there was no life.
Where the world was flat and angular, suddenly
it is round, like an orange.

In one corner the Macondo sun shines
brilliantly on a woman with shoes the colour
of old silver and a hat made of tiny flowers.
She browses near a man who moves among the shelves
systematically, serenely, running his hands
over covers and titles in the same parsimonious way
he papered his house with banknotes.

Elsewhere, a cast of characters become complete,
three-dimensional and disgraceful in a faded front room,
answering their own distressing questions.

Though outside it is raining and unspectacular,
inside (somewhere in the stopover between
being and oblivion) there is lightness and weight,
soul and body, words misunderstood –
for nothing more than the turn of a page.

Rebecca Perry

Contents

Contents

bookshops are
time machines
spaceships
story-makers
secret-keepers
dragon-tamers
dream-catchers
fact-finders
& safe places.

*(this book is for those
who know this to be true)*

A BRIEF HISTORY:
THE WORLD OF BOOKS

Bookshops are full of stories. Not just stories on shelves, but those hidden away. There are the stories of bookshop owners, and all the books they read that made them fall in love with reading. There are the stories of authors, and why they wrote their first book. There are the stories of second-hand books, and all the people who owned them. And there's the story of every single customer who walks through the door. We all love stories, with their sense of mystery and adventure.

At the antiquarian bookshop where I work part-time, a little girl once told me she loves bookshops because they are houses for stories. Another asked if she could get to Narnia through one of the bookcases. A young boy suggested I get a dragon to guard all the books in the shop when I wasn't there. When I asked him if that mightn't be a fire hazard, he rolled his eyes and told me that *obviously* I'd have to get a *trained* one.

Sadly I'm yet to find a bookshop dragon, let alone a trained one, but it's true that stories have always been associated with magic. Some of the earliest writing ever found, in southern Iraq from 4,000 BC, was used to record horoscopes. Archaeologists have also found Chinese writing on 50,000 tortoise shells, called Oracle Bones, on which shamans would carve questions before examining them by firelight as an early form of divination.

I've never written on shells myself and, despite a strong desire to work at Flourish and Blotts, I don't think I'm a witch, but when I was much younger I loved writing short stories *about* witches, sometimes on tree leaves using gel pens. I also remember writing secret notes using lemon juice as invisible ink – something I'd learnt from Enid Blyton. To make the writing visible you'd have to iron the paper and, as no parent's going to let their child use an iron, it wasn't so much invisible ink as impossible ink, but it was still fun. When I was twelve I moved on to machinery, writing a biography of my dead hamster on a ridiculously loud type-writer that would drive my parents mad as I powered on late into the night, the sound of typing punctured by gasps whenever my fingers got jammed between the keys. I thought the story was a masterpiece and secretly posted the manuscript off to Penguin in the hope they might publish it. (Wisely, they didn't).

We've written tales on many things over the past few thousand years: stone tablets, ivory, tree bark, palm leaves... Historians have even discovered copies of *The Iliad* and *The Odyssey* written out on the dried skins of serpents. The Ancient Romans used the inner bark of trees to write on, a peel called *liber*, which in turn became the Latin word *libri*, meaning book, and subsequently *livre, libro* and *library.* The Ancient Greeks wrote on parchment, the Egyptians on papyrus; the Chinese invention of paper didn't reach Europe for nearly a thousand years.

In the Ancient world, most books were read out in public by would-be writers – the notion of silent reading came much later – and if an audience approved, it was likely that a patron would pay to have the author's work copied out by slaves. Such patrons were the first publishers, and the book stalls they would set up near temples and in the food markets of central town squares were the first bookshops.

By the 1400s books were being created by carving a print block out of a huge chunk of wood, dipping it into ink and pressing it onto paper – a very inefficient method, because the block would often break. But in 1450, when Johann Gutenberg developed a moving printing press in Germany that enabled books to be produced faster and more cheaply, literacy was able to spread to the masses. Vespasiano da Bisticci, a famous bookseller in Florence, was so outraged that books would no longer be written out by hand that he closed his bookshop in a fit of rage, and became the first person in history to prophesy the death of the book industry.

So what about the booksellers and bookshops who didn't throw their toys out of their prams? Bookshops as physical places only became prevalent from the 1500s onwards. For thousands of years before, travelling booksellers went from town to town selling books. (See the booksellers of Montereggio on page 151, and the Bouquinistes in Paris on page 111). The first mention of a bookseller setting up a bookshop permanently in London is recorded as late as 1311. The early booksellers often sold other wares too, such as fabrics and plain parchment, and with the invention of the moving printing press they took on the role of bookbinders, often designing bespoke book covers for customers with their initials embossed on the cloth which, for a premium, could be dyed a particular colour.

We've now reached the twenty-first century through a period of intense change for the book industry in recent years, with the rise of chain bookshops soon followed by their swift decline, the exponential growth of online shopping and the invention of the e-reader. So much has changed, indeed, that a lot of people have again been asking: are physical books and bookshops still relevant? But when so much of our lives is spent on computers, dealing with concepts and files that we can't actually hold in our hands, the idea of a shopping experience, and of a physical book, is perhaps more important than ever before.

Running a bookshop is no easy task: some are closing due to increased rents, business rates, and retail giants undercutting prices – but I think we forget that it's always been a challenge. Think of the travelling book-sellers who walked, carrying books, for hundreds of miles; think of monks who, a thousand years ago, had to handwrite every single book; think of the fight for freedom of speech and freedom of information – still a very real battle in many parts of the world today.

In response to all these challenges, bookshops across the globe are cer-tainly showing what they're made of. In April 2014 Sanlian Taofen Bookstore in Beijing opened its first twenty-four-hour bookstore, gen-erating a massive boost in sales. Book Towns are sprouting up all over the world, to save local economies and form stronger communities. At the Winter Conference of the American Booksellers Association in early 2014, its CEO Oren Teicher reported that sales of e-books were starting to plateau and that many independent bookshops in the States had their best ever Christmas. Philip Jones, the editor of the *Bookseller* magazine in the UK, is confident that proactive independent bookshops have the room and potential to continue to grow. It's an exciting time for bookshops: they're fighting harder than perhaps they've ever had to; consequently they've become more inventive than they've ever had to be.

As for me, I've moved on from writing books about my dead hamster. I've worked in bookshops for seven years now, with new and old books, in England and in Scotland, and find them to be magical places, instilling a sense of wonder and adventure in children, and offering a haven in a busy world for all of us to stop and think. They are portals to infinite possibility and they are, as that little girl once said to me, houses for stories.

Stories connect people: I want to share the stories of three hundred wonderful bookshops across six continents, and thoughts from famous authors about their favourite bookshops, too. These days, we've got booksellers in cities, in deserts, and in the middle of a rain forest; we've got travelling bookshops, and bookshops underground. We've got bookshops in barns, in caravans and in converted Victorian railway stations. We've even got booksellers selling books in the middle of a war.

Are bookshops still relevant? They certainly are.

All bookshops are full of stories, and stories want to be heard.

BOOKSHOPS AROUND THE WORLD & THOUGHTS FROM THOSE WHO LOVE THEM

Europe

Set aglow by the setting sun, the magic of The Bookshop was on display. Dark wooden shelves stuffed with books surrounded me as the room opened into a large gallery. My nostrils were filled with the musky aroma of old pages and dust. There were original fireplaces set into the walls, hardwood floors that seemed to stretch on and on, chandeliers overhead, and, in the shadows of the evening, I could see that there were little trinkets and treasures everywhere... Oil paintings rested against the walls while random antiques – a bowler hat here or a stuffed pheasant there – were artfully and often humorously set on display. Through another doorway, past the Children's section and into a long hall, Euan pointed above me and I looked up to see a skeleton hanging from the ceiling, playing the violin...

As we continued further in, rooms opened on to each other, each with its own character. The Transportation Room was a small stone room off the main hall filled with books on transportation of all kinds. Under the room's wooden floor Euan opened a trap door to reveal a working model train, which rode through a replica of Wigtown's square – it was so secret and hidden that no one would have known it was there... The hall then led to a door into a garden, where there was a small stone building aptly named the Garden Room, stuffed with more books and antiques...

It was, indeed, the ideal bookshop.

from *Three Things You Need to Know*
About Rockets by Jessica A. Fox

Scotland

◆

Wigtown

On the west coast of Scotland, surrounded by salt marsh and forest, you'll find Wigtown. Known as the National Book Town of Scotland, it's also a place where everyone (quite charmingly) knows everyone else's business. It has a population of just one thousand and, when I arrived in 2012, ten people approached me within half an hour asking if I'd met Shaun Bythell yet. Shaun is a bit of a local legend. He runs the largest bookshop in Wigtown – in fact, The Bookshop is the largest second-hand bookshop in Scotland – and for some time he had, as these people kept telling me, been wanting to write a book like my own (*Weird Things Customers Say in Bookshops*). Their advice was to keep my head down and avoid him, because he was apparently quite annoyed that I'd got there first. Not wanting to become the most hated woman in Wigtown or be chased down the street by an angry Scottish bookseller, I spent my first day rummaging through Wigtown's other bookshops instead, because there are quite a few of those.

Back in the day, Wigtown used to be on the railway, but the line closed in the 1960s and led to the decline of the town's main employer, the Bladnoch Creamery. A decade later John Carter, a jeweller based in nearby Newton Stewart, was burgled. He wasn't insured, and couldn't afford to re-stock his shop, so he decided to sell cheaper products instead: he decided to sell books. Over the next thirty years the bookshop grew, and relocated to Wigtown's town square, where it became The Bookshop. With work in the town still short, and the success of the now very large bookshop, the folk of Wigtown got together and put in a bid to become Scotland's 'National Book Town'. Five other towns were also bidding for the chance to become the Hay-on-Wye of Scotland (see page 102) – to hopefully share the success of the little town near the Welsh border, whose fortunes had been transformed by its remarkable number of bookshops. Wigtown won, and a call was put out to book-sellers and book-lovers across the country: *Come on an adventure with us – move here and open a bookshop!*

And people came. Moira McCarty moved her bookshop down from the Orkneys; Richard and Marion van de Voort transported their science fiction bookshop from London to Scotland; Angela Everitt came from the north-east of England to set up a feminist bookshop and café. Scotland's National Book Town became a big success. Bookshops opened up and down the main square, in warehouses, and in people's living rooms. Wigtown went a step further: it launched an annual book festival. Every autumn for a week and a half, the literati of the UK and beyond descend, and festival organisers, booksellers, bed-and-breakfast owners, authors, readers and volunteers work around the clock to put on 200 book events in just ten days. It's brilliant – and utterly mad.

So that's how I came to know Wigtown – doing a book talk during festival season. It has two dozen book businesses, from bookshops to book binders and publishers – the Box of Frogs, the Old Bank, Book Corner, Byre Books in a barn filled with wonderfully obscure books on myths and fairy tales – and after a cheerful festival volunteer had driven me the fifty-four miles from the nearest railway station at Dumfries, telling me proudly all about his family heritage, about all the famous authors he'd chauffeured around, and how Wigtown is perfect for star-gazing because it has the darkest skies in Europe, I set out to explore as many of these bookshops as I could.

My first port of call was ReadingLasses Bookshop & Café. There aren't many things in life better than books, tea and cake (if you disagree, I'm afraid we can never be friends), and at ReadingLasses, where you can get all three at the same time, you soon lose any desire to leave. Not to mention the fact that they have an excellent bookshop dog: a spaniel, who goes by the name of Rupert Earl O' the Machars.

'Susan and I bought the shop with the aim of making it a place where people can come and just *be*,' said Rupert's owner, Gerrie Douglas-Scott.

'There's space to work; there's space to read; there's space to eat, and we even have "Rooms Above the Books" for people to stay.'

Gerrie doesn't just run the bookshop: she's also a Humanist Celebrant – so when she's not organising author events or buying in books she's whizzing around the south-west of Scotland performing weddings, often on windswept beaches. Indeed, she adds, 'We've done three weddings actually inside the bookshop. At the end of the ceremony I get the town buildings to ring their bells, and then a local piper comes in and we all have a party. There's something very moving about it.' As she said this, I resolved immediately to get married inside a bookshop one day, and berated myself for never having thought of it before. As Gerrie says: 'Who wouldn't want to get married in a room full of love stories?'

Several books heavier and contemplating leaving London for the west coast of Scotland, I went on to the Wigtown Book Festival opening party. We were huddled in a tent, rain was falling, there were questions over whether the fireworks would work, and despite advice from the local population, I managed to run straight into Shaun. Shaun-who-apparently-didn't-like-me-Shaun. Red-faced and embarrassed, I found myself stammering a lot and offering profuse apologies for having written a book called *Weird Things Customers Say in Bookshops* before he had. Shaun raised an eyebrow and grinned. 'I don't know if you've heard, Jen, but I'm too bloody grumpy to pull off a book like that.' Then he handed me a gin and tonic.

And just like that, he became one of my favourite booksellers.

Shaun bought The Bookshop from John Carter nearly fifteen years ago. The place is huge: it has over a mile of shelving, with some 100,000 books. When he took the bookshop on, none of the shelves had been made to fit, and 'everything was a little wonky.' Doors between the different rooms meant that customers thought they weren't allowed to go through into the other sections, so Shaun got rid of these as soon as possible: 'Unfortunately, opening the place up means the bookshop is now bloody freezing,' he says. '…but then this is Scotland.' There's an old fireplace next to the poetry shelves, a transport section with a model railway running under the floorboards, and a bookshop cat that quite often runs away from home. Those who have read the (rather suspicious-looking) rave online reviews of The Bookshop's delicious lobster bisque and seafood platter might be a little disappointed to find out that it serves neither of these things (in fact it doesn't have a café at all) – but it does have an owner with a slightly wicked sense of humour who enjoys spending time on TripAdvisor. One of Shaun's latest projects is the Random Book Club, where customers anywhere in the world can pay an annual fee to have a random second-hand book delivered to their door every month. After fourteen years of selling books, the main thing Shaun says he has learned is that anyone who comes in asking for books in a foreign language is just showing off: 'They never buy anything. And we have a pretty good stock of foreign nonsense.'

Shaun's house is actually attached to the bookshop. A staircase is roped off with a sign saying 'Private', but during the festival he opens his doors and the rooms overflow with writers and artists in various stages of ine-briation. He has also, as a nod to Shakespeare and Company (see page 112), built a mezzanine floor in the middle of the shop with a double bed so people can stay during the festival. 'One day a woman came in and wanted to book the place for the Tuesday,' Shaun tells me.

'I told her we'd all be out that night at the Literary Pub Quiz, but to let herself in at the side door. Well, I completely forgot she was coming. We all came back from the quiz and at about 2 a.m. when I was sorting out where everyone could sleep, I said to an author, "Oh, you can go and sleep in the bed in the bookshop!" and off he went. The poor bloke climbed into the bed, and the poor lady sat up straight and hit him, crying: "I beg your pardon! I've paid twenty quid to sleep here!"'

The other question I was asked when I visited Wigtown, alongside 'Have you met Shaun yet?' was 'Have you met Jessica Fox?' At first, I had no idea who this was. 'She's away at the moment,' they said. 'You must come back when she's here!' 'She's American, you know. She's so full of energy.' One lady even beckoned me close, so she could whisper in my ear: 'Jessica used to work at NASA… and she does something called yoga!' Each time someone mentioned her, I grew more intrigued.

Jessica, I discovered, had indeed worked for NASA. She's also a film-maker, and had always dreamed of visiting a second-hand bookshop in Scotland. One day, dissatisfied with life in LA, she opened her laptop and Googled 'used bookshop, Scotland'. Shaun's bookshop was the first link to appear. Nervous, but imagining walls lined with books right next to the sea, Jessica sent him an email asking if she could travel 5,000 miles to try her hand at being a bookseller, in his shop, for a month, for free.

The response from Shaun came back half an hour later: 'Tell me a bit about yourself.'

So she did. They talked and, a few months later, Jessica packed up her bags and flew from LA all the way to Scotland. Thus began their book-shop love story, filled with windswept castles, woolly jumpers and grumpy bookshop-keeping. (Think *84, Charing Cross Road* but with email and fewer powdered eggs). It certainly proves Gerrie's theory about bookshops being romantic places. If you want to know the full story, you can check out Jessica's book *Three Things You Need to Know About Rockets*.

◆

The Edinburgh Bookshop

My first job as a bookseller was at the Edinburgh Bookshop in Scotland. I grew up near Newcastle in the north-east of England, where there was, and still is, a sad lack of independent bookshops. So when I went to university in Edinburgh, I was amazed by how many bookshops the city had, and proceeded to explore them all. There's the wonderfully named Elvis Shakespeare, a book and record shop down Leith Walk; the Gently Mad, a bookshop and bookbinder on Summer Place; Le Troubadour, an antiquarian bookshop owned by a man called Aeneas who previously ran an organic farm and weaving mill on the Isle of Mull; and McNaughtan's Bookshop, which doubles as an art gallery, and was set up in 1957 by a major who had retired from the army. A local favourite of mine was Till's, just around the corner from the university campus, a fantastic secondhand bookshop run by a friendly guy from Canada – more than anything I remember the smell of the place: a mixture of dust, vanilla and the kind of paper that's been hiding stories for hundreds of years.

However, it was the Edinburgh Bookshop that pulled me in most. Set in the heart of Bruntsfield, it was opened eight years ago by Vanessa and Malcolm Robertson, and is now run by Marie Moser. Vanessa also runs Fidra, a small publishing company that specialises in rescuing neglected children's books – I was an intern there before moving into the shop itself. It was the final year of my English Literature degree, and considering I spent most of my free time haunting bookshops it seemed prudent to try and be paid to spend time in one.

The Edinburgh Bookshop is a small but beautifully formed space, and I loved spending my Saturdays recommending books to local families. At the time we had a bookshop dog called Teaga, a huge, friendly Leonberger who was adored by everyone, especially the postman (yes, really). Somehow we managed to convince most of the children that Teaga was actually Nana from *Peter Pan*. They'd look at her furry form in amazement and ask if they could ride her.

❖

Bookish Fact

Lignin, an organic polymer found in trees, is chemically similar to vanillin, the primary extract of the vanilla bean. So when trees are made into books and kept for long periods of time, the lignin in the paper breaks down and starts to smell like vanilla.

This is why antiquarian books, and second-hand bookshops, smell so damn good.

I soon learned that parents would leave their children in the shop and disappear across the road to Tesco; that toddlers thought themselves ninjas and would try to climb the shelves; that middle-aged women would break down in tears if we didn't have the latest *Twilight* book in stock. This is all part of the job.

We also had enthusiastic local authors, who would pop in to say hello, and J.K. Rowling spent her days writing in the café next door. (She complimented my skirt once; it made my year.) When Independent Booksellers' Week introduced an event called Strictly Come Bookselling, to get authors into bookshops and make them booksellers for the day, it led to several local authors visiting the Edinburgh Bookshop to do just that. One of those authors is Ian Rankin. Another is Vivian French. I had a chat with them about why they love books, and why they think bookshops are important places.

• A CHAT WITH IAN RANKIN •

Ian Rankin is the Edinburgh-based author of the Inspector Rebus series, which has sold in the tens of millions around the world. His website is ianrankin.net and you can follow him on Twitter where he is @beathhigh

" The first things I remember reading were comics. All the great comics that D.C. Thomson produced: the *Beano*, and the *Dandy*, and then the ones that were targeted at boys, the *Victor* and the *Hotspur.* I read them and I just got obsessed with storytelling.

There weren't many books in our house. My parents weren't great readers but we did have a local library. I would haunt that place. I'd take out the maximum number of books I could, and the biggest thrill for me was when they said: 'OK, Ian, you're now allowed to go into the adult section.' I must have been about eleven or twelve at the time. The thing was, we had a cinema in our town, but because of the film classifications I wasn't allowed to go and see the films I had an interest in seeing. But nobody stopped me reading the books. So books were exciting. They were taboo. They represented things the adult world didn't really want me to see. When I was twelve, my Christmas present list included things like *The Godfather* and *One Flew Over the Cuckoo's Nest*, because I knew they were films I wasn't old enough to go and see. Anything that was a 15 or 18 certificate, I would go and get the books, thinking 'A-ha! Here's something the grown-ups don't want me to know about!' Books were my way in.

As for bookshops, there wasn't one in our village, but there was a newsagents with a rack of paperbacks. So I would go in there and flick through those. I'd read thrillers by Alistair MacLean, who I didn't even realise was Scottish at the time: he wrote these big American-style thrillers and yet he was a native Gaelic speaker. Later I read Robert Ludlum, Frederick Forsyth... it was the usual *Boys' Own* stories, really, but it was something that I could share with my dad. On the rare occasions when he did read a book, in the summer holidays, it would always be a thriller, so it was a way of cementing our relationship.

The first real bookshop I visited was in Kirkcaldy, which was about half an hour away on the bus. They had a John Menzies there, which was the Scottish equivalent of W.H. Smith, but when I was fifteen a proper bookshop opened: one that only sold books, and it was exciting because it sold literature, not just the bestsellers. You could go there and get the collected poems of Thomas Hardy, which I did. Though the first book I bought was actually Alexander Solzhenitsyn's *The Gulag Archipelago, Volume Two*, which is slightly strange, I know. People had talked about him on TV, and I thought: 'I have to buy this big fat book by this famous author, in this new bookshop,' so I did. I never finished it. I probably still have it somewhere.

Now, living in Edinburgh, I can see the bookselling world has changed a bit. There used to be two big independent bookshops, family-owned: Thin's and Bauermeister's. When I was a student my girlfriend worked at Bauermeister's, so I got a discount there, which was great. Both of those shops have gone now, though Thin's has been taken over by Blackwell's. I suppose the bookshop scene has contracted, but the good news is that a few bookshops have opened in Edinburgh in the past few years, including the Edinburgh Bookshop and Looking Glass Books. We've still got Waterstones, of course, and Blackwell's, and we've got lots of second-hand bookshops, too.

The thing is, Edinburgh is still a city of literature. It's a city that prides itself on the number of writers who have come from here, or who still work here. It's got a big university, a big English Literature department; it's got a captive audience of readers. The book festival is great, though it's only two or three weeks of the year, and the UNESCO City of Literature put on as many events as they can, and get-togethers for writers as well. It's certainly lively.

I took part in The Edinburgh Bookshop's Strictly Come Bookselling one year, and I could hardly get near the till because the other authors enjoyed it so much. I think Maggie O'Farrell came in for a while, and Vivian French and Sara Sheridan gave it a go, too. It was fun, but it's hard work, though I knew that from when my girlfriend worked at Bauermeister's.

There are many books I'd love to recommend if I worked in bookselling. I always recommend *The Prime of Miss Jean Brodie* by Muriel Spark to people, especially those who aren't great readers, as it's only 125 pages, so it's not going to put anyone off. It packs a lot in, though. It's funny and it's sad; it's complex and it's poetic. It's very Edinburgh, too.

I've been to many different bookshops on tour. Powell's in Portland, Oregon is always great fun (see page 186). It's a whole city block, a huge bookshop, and they've got pretty much anything you could ever want. It's a great place to browse as well as do events. It used to be the case, when I went to America, that every small town had an independent bookstore that specialised in crime. There used to be five or six in New York alone, and now I think there's only one left. Where possible, I always try and visit crime bookshops that still exist. There's one in Belfast called No Alibis, and of course we crime writers do have festivals and conferences where authors and readers can meet.

As a reader, I think bookshops are important because nothing beats the experience of browsing. You cannot replicate it online. In a well-run bookshop you are always going to find something that you want to read. If not, hopefully you can chat with the bookseller and they will tell you about something you didn't know existed. You get that personal recommendation. You build up a relationship.

As for bookshops and children, I was just in the Edinburgh Bookshop last week when they were doing story-time for toddlers. The bookseller sits on the floor, with all the kids around, and they read together. It's just brilliant. Although my kids are grown up now, I know all about taking your kids into bookshops and their excitement at finding some fantastic story with great illustrations, or something that's got daft rhymes – it makes reading fun for them. They discover the stories, and you get to buy them for them and take them home. Then when you read them together you get just as much enjoyment out of it as they do.

Just a few days ago I was up in Perth visiting my sister. Her grand-daughter was there; she's two years old and she'd received a lot of books for Christmas. All she wanted to do was sit up in an armchair and have me read the stories to her. It was a hoot. It just brought it all back, really. I remembered reading *Green Eggs and Ham* to my son when he was little, and before that reading the crime books with my dad over the summer holidays. It would be a very sad world without bookshops and literacy. Literacy is a ladder: just as comics took me to books, children's stories take you to adult stories. Hopefully parents help their children build up a passion for reading, a passion for knowledge, and a passion for entertainment.

As a writer, bookshops are a huge connection between you and your readers. You bump into readers when you're book shopping, and they say 'Oh, I loved your last book: could you sign a book for me? Could you sign a book for my friend? Could you sign a book for my granny?' Good bookshops put on events which connect writers with the public, but they're also places I go to to buy books for research. While I'm there I also get to eye up the competition. I get to go into the shop and think, 'How dare they have so many Norwegian crime novels?' and then cheekily place my own books on top of them. You can always tell, when you're travelling, which authors have been through the airport bookshops before you, because their books are the ones facing out on all the shelves.

If I could open any kind of bookshop, and sell anything I liked, I'd have to open a multi-media bookshop. I'd sell music books, but I'd also sell vinyl. There'd be live music from singer-songwriters, and a little café, too. I'd sit behind my desk with my feet up, and I wouldn't give a damn if I didn't sell anything. I would be playing my music. See, I'd be like Bernard Black. I'd read the books I wanted to read, sell the books I wanted to sell, play the music I wanted to play. And if nobody else liked my bookshop, they could go stuff themselves. ,,

❖

BOOKISH FACT

The word abibliophobia (noun)
is the fear of running out of
things to read.

• A CHAT WITH VIVIAN FRENCH •

Vivian French was best known in school for being extremely skinny and talking a lot. There she developed an attachment to words and later became an actor, then a storyteller, and finally a writer of children's books. She is the author of more than two hundred books. She lives in Edinburgh, and has four grown-up daughters.

" I've done three separate days of Strictly Come Bookselling with the Edinburgh Bookshop over the past few years, and I've loved all of them. I took part with various lovely authors, including Ian Rankin, Maggie O'Farrell, Lari Don and Sara Sheridan. It's enough to make you realise just how hard booksellers work – it's not about sitting around smiling, hoping people will buy things. Oh, no. And I love recommending books to people – although of course you do feel that responsibility to find them something they're going to really treasure.

As for me, I love some of the more unknown, quirky books, and I'm a sucker for humour. It's also fun to recommend books that have been around for quite a long time, and that people might have missed; that way it feels as though you're playing a role in breathing life back into the story. Almost as though you're part of it. Generally I'm a big fan of the Persephone classics (see page 95) and I actually managed to persuade three people to buy them whilst trying my hand at bookselling. My favourite is *Miss Ranskill Comes Home*. All of them are beautifully made.

As a parent, and as a children's author, I particularly think it's wonderful to let children loose in a bookshop; to let them look at the books, feel them and, most importantly, *smell* them. My oldest daughter, when she was four, used to carry around a very small edition of Julius Caesar's *The Gallic Wars,* and she took it wherever she went. Of course, she couldn't read it. She just knew that books were good, and she liked this particular one because of the way it felt in her hand. And because she could hug it.

If I opened up my own bookshop, I think I would mainly stock children's books. There would be tea and cake, and lots of comfy chairs so customers could stay a while and make sure they'd found *just the right book* before buying it. I'd call my shop something like 'The Powerhouse' because I really do believe that words are the most powerful things in the world.

I noticed, working at the Edinburgh Bookshop, that sometimes people would come in and you could be quite sure they were there because it was pouring down with rain outside, and they had very little intention of buying anything. In those cases, I loved slowly starting to engage with them, in a non-pushy way, and just having a friendly chat. Normally this led to us talking about books, which of course we were surrounded by, and often I or another bookseller was then able to recommend a book so perfect that they were determined to buy it. I enjoyed chatting to people like this; it's no use trying to push books on people. You can't tell old ladies of ninety-two that they're going to love *The Hunger Games*, can you?

I'm so local to the Edinburgh Bookshop that when I stop by these days I often find myself enthusiastically recommending things to people, and you can see the customers thinking 'Who *is* this woman?' I suppose I am guilty of getting a bit carried away – but that's what one does, you see, when one loves books so very much! **"**

◆

Loch Croispol Bookshop, Durness

In May 2013, the most remote bookshop in the UK went up for sale. Kevin and his partner Simon have run the bookshop and its restaurant, tucked up in the far north-western corner of Scotland, for the past fourteen years. It's definitely remote (the nearest hospital is a hundred miles away), and sometimes it can be hard to get supplies, but its setting on the rugged Sutherland coast beside the sea is the perfect place to read a book. At the time of writing, it still hasn't been bought. So, if anyone fancies it...

◆

Far From the Madding Crowd, Linlithgow

Jill Pattle's bookshop confirms a suspicion I've had for a long time: that events in bookshops are more of a success when cake is involved. Far From the Madding Crowd has put on all kinds of events over the years, often involving baking. 'We had our famous Harry Potter book launches,' Jill tells me. 'Midnight feasts on the pavements with Cauldron Cakes. We had a huge queue and lots of dressing-up was involved. We even had real owls to keep us company, including a gorgeous snowy owl, who fell asleep on his handler's arm because it was past his bedtime! Where else would you have an event like that, in the middle of the night in a wee high street, but in an independent bookshop!'

◆

The Watermill, Aberfeldy

Ten years ago, Jayne and Kevin Ramage decided to leave London to set up a bookshop in Scotland. They found a run-down oatmeal mill in the middle of Perthshire, and have transformed it into three floors of books, an art gallery, a homeware section and a café. During the winter, the Watermill has had customers turn up to the bookshop on skis, and the biggest event they've ever done was in a local Scottish castle. Though Kevin admits that the e-reader has its place, he and Jayne go hiking in the Alps for three weeks every year, carrying the whole world on their backs, or 10 kg each, to be precise – 3 kg of which is books. (If you want more book-related exercise, check out John Green's video 'Fitness for Nerds' on YouTube.)

The Watermill is so large that there's a square foot of bookshop for every person in their town. 'It's a Grade I listed building,' Kevin says. 'But when we bought it, the insides had been taken over by the rain and the rats. We saw the potential, though, and the rest is history. I used to run the Owl Bookshop in Kentish Town, and whilst I enjoyed that, running a bookshop in London is very restricted when it comes to space, as rent is so high. Where we are now, we can allow books to breathe. We can put them face out; we can show them off to their best potential. We've been able to enter into the theatre of bookselling. Michael Palin opened the bookshop for us. It was a beautiful day, and he was stood on a *Romeo and Juliet*-style balcony, just off the children's section, looking out over the car park, making a speech, and we were all below, listening. It was a very "Friends, Romans, countrymen!" type of affair.'

◆

The Mainstreet Trading Company, St Boswells

Just before we disappear over the Scottish border to look at bookshops in England, we need to talk about the Mainstreet Trading Company. I first met its owner Rosamund de la Hey five years ago; she was the children's marketing director at Bloomsbury, and had decided to leave life in the Big Smoke to open a bookshop and café in an old auction house in Scotland, along with her husband Bill, a chef.

Since opening, they've expanded into a barn in the courtyard outside their bookshop and have a deli (opened by Tom Kitchin) and a homeware section, and in 2012 were voted Independent Bookseller of the Year. Did I mention they also sell cheese? And the bookshop has two wonderful 'Book Burrows' tucked under the stairs, like Harry Potter bedrooms, where children can go to read and listen to audiobooks. Rosamund and the staff even created tiny homes, with Borrowers in them, hidden under the floorboards for customers to peer into.

'It's all about the intimacy of books,' Rosamund tells me. 'Bookshops are evolving. We're now stronger, better and more focused than ever before

❖

BOOKISH FACT

The Klencke Atlas is one of the world's largest atlases, created in 1660 by the Dutch prince John Maurice of Nassau. Containing three dozen maps measuring nearly 6 foot by 6 foot, it requires six people to lift it. The book was a present for Charles II to mark the occasion of his restoration to the throne, and was said to contain all the geographical knowledge of the time. Today you can find it in the antiquarian mapping section of the British Library in London.

For 350 years this was the largest atlas in the world, until the creation of *Earth Platinum* in 2012 by the Australian publisher Millennium House. This book is bigger by a whole foot, and contains the world's largest image in a book, a photograph of the Shanghai skyline. It is 272 gigapixels and made up of more than 12,000 images put together.

– building on our community and our environment. We always keep in touch with our local bookshops – some of our favourites are Cogito Books in Hexham, and Forum Books in Corbridge.' Teaming up with eight other bookshop owners, the Mainstreet Trading Company have set up the Borders Book Trail, producing a beautiful map and booklet to help tourists at the Borders Book Festival find local literary hotspots.

'Our bookshop's fifth birthday party is probably my favourite memory,' says Rosamund. 'We themed it so children could dress up as their favourite characters but, unprompted, our staff turned up in fancy dress too. It was very funny. The best part was when Maggie O'Farrell and her husband, writer William Sutcliffe, *and* their three children turned up, all dressed up as characters from *Alice in Wonderland*. We hadn't asked them to do that, either. Clearly all of us want to disappear into books, and then bring them to life... in a very visual way!'

• A CHAT WITH KIRSTY LOGAN •

Kirsty Logan's first book, *The Rental Heart and Other Fairytales*, is published by Salt. Her debut novel, *The Gracekeepers,* will be published in Spring 2015.

❝ I grew up in bookshops. My mother was a bookseller, and I'd help out with stock-takes, unpacking, and dressing up as characters from children's books for reading events – always requesting my payment in books. At sixteen I got a Sunday job in a bookshop; summers and Christmases were spent full-time among the shelves. Teenage years are some of the hardest of our lives, but those years among books helped me through. In any chaos, there was always comfort in stories: they took me out of myself and helped me understand who I was and who I wanted to be. Whatever your problems, a book is a point where you can stop in a moving world. **❞**

England

♦

Barter Books, Alnwick, Northumberland

Once upon a time, there was a man from England who loved trains, and a woman from America who loved books. They met on a transatlantic flight, and only started talking because he passed her a handwritten note saying hello.

Three years later Stuart and Mary got married, and decided to combine their main interests in life. They opened a bookshop inside a Victorian railway station in the north of England, and they called it Barter Books. It started off small, in just one of the seven rooms available, but it grew. And then it grew some more. Now it's one of the largest second-hand bookshops in Europe and, amazingly, one of the main employers in its town. There aren't many bookshops that can say that. With lines of poetry written along its shelves, and model trains running along the top of the bookcases, it's a bit of a booklover's dream. The old Waiting Room has a coal fire, the old Manager's Office has become a tea room, and there are sofas tucked in between the shelves for you to sit down and read. They've even commissioned artists to decorate the walls.

There is something else special about this bookshop. With the Second World War about to break out, and public morale all-important, the British government commissioned three propaganda posters. In the summer of 1939 two of these posters went into circulation, and could be found in shop windows across the UK. 'Freedom is in Peril!' said one; the other, 'Your Courage, Your Cheerfulness, Your Resolution will bring us victory!' The third poster was kept back, intended to be distributed if air raids further dampened people's spirits. In the end it was never sent out, and hardly anyone saw it.

In 2000, Stuart and Mary Manley bought a box of books for their shop at an auction. At the bottom of the box they found a dust-covered poster. It said, 'Keep Calm and Carry On.' This was what the third poster had said. A pretty good message for a bookseller, really. Stuart liked it, and so did Mary, so they framed it and put it up on a wall in Barter Books. 'Keep Calm And Carry On.' It turned out they weren't the only ones who liked the poster. It attracted so much attention from customers that a year later they decided to start producing facsimile copies to sell. With the history behind the poster unearthed, the phrase 'Keep Calm and Carry On' went viral. Printed on posters, mugs, cards and T-shirts, it became one of the first crazes of the twenty-first century, and spawned parodies all over the world. These included some of my favourites: 'Keep Calm and... Expecto Patronum!' and, of course, 'Keep Calm and Read a Book.' Sound advice if ever there was any.

◆

The Old Pier Bookshop, Morecambe

The Old Pier Bookshop on the seafront in Morecambe is a second-hand and antiquarian bookshop owned by Tony Vettese. If any bookshop was a Tardis, it's this one. It's full to the brim and, though it might not appear to have any order to it, Tony knows where everything is. 'I've always wanted a bookshop,' says Tony. 'I came from a virtually illiterate household, and my first book was put into my hands by an excellent primary school teacher. My parents opened a chip shop in Morecambe next to the pier, but when the pier closed down, the restaurant couldn't survive any more. So I started selling books in the café instead, and gradually the books took over.'

During the first five years of the bookshop, Tony worked as a taxi driver to help keep the business afloat. Now people come to visit from all over the country, and the books have taken over the entire ground floor of the building – including old store rooms and cupboards. It's an amazing bookish maze. 'I have to stop and imagine what it was like without the bookcases, and all the shelves, and all the panels,' Tony says. 'And I can't, really. I suppose I've got too many books, but how can you turn books away? You never know what's going to be at the bottom of the next box; you never know what you're going to find. Apart from a first edition of *The Hobbit* – and I took that home with me; I'm never going to sell that one – one day I found an original copy of Philip K. Dick's first book *World of Chance.*' Another fond memory is the customer who once asked if he had a copy of *Tess of the Gerbils*. 'Since opening the bookshop, I've become a calmer person, too. I used to be in the army, and my life was very hectic. Having the bookshop is wonderful. It's the best way to live your life, I think.'

Not only do you not know what books you're going to find, but you never know who's going to walk through the door, either. Eight years ago, a woman called Irena came into the Old Pier Bookshop, and she and Tony started talking. She was from Poland, visiting the UK, and she told him she'd only come so far north because she liked Celtic crosses. In fact, she was planning to go back to Poland to become a nun. But she and Tony fell in love, got married, and she didn't go back to Poland. She didn't become a nun, either.

• THOUGHTS FROM A BOOKSHOP CUSTOMER •

Josephine Wilkinson is a big fan of the Old Pier Bookshop:

" It's run by just one guy, and the first time we ever went in he told us his wife was due to give birth that day – yet there he was, selling books. The second time, a few months later, he had his son strapped to his chest – 'Start 'em early,' he said with a grin. There's a bookshop dog – naturally – and piles upon piles of books, so many piles that you're a little bit scared to go all the way in, in case one of those piles topples and you're trapped in there forever – although, actually, would that be such a terrible fate? There doesn't seem to be any kind of organisation to these piles, either; it's all incredibly haphazard.

I was looking for a copy of *Rebecca* once, for my Mum. I asked Tony (we called him Mr Bookshop) if he happened to have one,

❖

BOOKISH FACT

The name 'Wendy' used to be a boy's name, and in nineteenth-century censuses in both the US and UK it can only be found a handful of times for either gender. Previously there had been two Chinese emperors called Wendi, though the name is probably etymologically distinct. It was J.M. Barrie's play *Peter Pan* (1904) that made 'Wendy' a popular name for girls.

and it seemed like a fruitless request because there is no *way* he could know what books he has in the place, and even less chance of him being able to locate what he wanted. But he just smiled, quoted the first line to me and then made a sharp dip to his left, breathing in to squeeze between the shelves, running his fingers along the spines of the books four shelves up, before muttering 'Aha!' and pulling out a book halfway along. Behind it, totally hidden from view, was *Rebecca*. He didn't even hesitate; it's like he has some kind of connection to all the words that live under his roof. Our jaws dropped.

There are old annuals, and magazines; a massive shelf of children's literature; a whole room devoted to crime; a shelf right up at the top (which is where my crazy-tall brother comes in handy) full of gorgeous hardback editions of the classics; a cardboard box – a cardboard box! – full of little leather copies of Shakespeare from the late 1800s (I bought *Much Ado* for my granny) and these locked glass cabinets which can only be full of the 'good stuff.' Sometimes you have to climb over overflowing boxes to get into the little rooms created by all the shelves, and even though it looks tiny from the outside it's like a maze once you get in there. And it smells so good. It smells of old books and happy memories. **"**

Josephine Wilkinson lives in Lancashire and has promised her boyfriend that she's going to stop buying so many books. Some day. You can find her at *livetoreadreadtolive.blogspot.com*

• A CHAT WITH DAVID ALMOND •

David Almond is the author of *Skellig, The Boy Who Swam with Piranhas, The Tightrope Walkers* and many other novels, stories and plays. His major awards include the Carnegie Medal and the 2010 Hans Christian Andersen Award. He lives in Northumberland and is Professor of Creative Writing at Bath Spa University.

" One bookshop that jumps to mind straight away, and actually features in my novel *The Tightrope Walkers*, is Ultima Thule. I used to go there as a teenager in Newcastle in the 1970s. It was in the Handysides Arcade, alongside some cafés and alternative shops, and it was amazing. It was run by a poet and a novelist; they had a lot of American stock, and small press pamphlets, and were attached to the Morden Tower – an ancient turret in Newcastle's city walls where, for the past forty five years, hundreds of poets have come from all over the world to give poetry readings. Ultima Thule sold the kind of things you would only find going into a bookshop like that – literary magazines and small press stuff, and they'd based themselves on City Lights bookstore in San Francisco (see page 204). Allen Ginsberg even came to the bookshop once. I remember thinking how impressive it was that a kid from Tyneside had gone into a bookshop where Allen Ginsberg had stood. That was a really important place when I was a kid, aspiring to be a writer.

The library was very important to me as a kid, too – a little branch that was just down the street from where we lived. I had an uncle who printed a newspaper, as well, and so I fell in love with the printed page when I was just a baby, really. It seemed amazing to me – the beauty of print on paper. That itself inspired me to be a writer, as well as books themselves, and stories. The way adults would tell stories around me, and tell jokes and sing songs, it seemed that the thing for me to do was to put the two things together and write them down.

We didn't have loads of books in our house, but I remember the thrill of getting books on Christmas morning. Taking a book out of a Christmas stocking, slightly curved, and when you flattened it out and opened it you saw this beautiful print, and sometimes a fantastic illustration to go with it. It was that sense of surprise and the beauty of the book as an object.

I remember when Waterstones came to Newcastle for the first time, and the sense of excitement that came with it. We didn't have a general bookshop before they came, just specialist stuff, and then here was this new place with four floors crammed full of books. I don't remember the first book I bought, but I do remember being interested in parapsychology, and the paranormal, and trying to find books on that kind of stuff. There weren't many around, but when I was thirteen I bought *The Third Eye* by Lobsang Rampa.

These days we've got a great bookshop here in Hexham called Cogito Books. It's a fantastically well-run shop – one of those places where you don't really know what you're looking for, but you walk in and there it is, waiting for you. Foyles are also doing some amazing stuff at the moment. They're being very optimistic about the whole book world, and have recreated themselves, which seems very positive and progressive. [See page 87]

I've been to some wonderful places on book tour, too. Books of Wonder in New York is fantastic, and City Lights bookstore in San Francisco was a real thrill for me to go to, having admired it from thousands of miles away as a kid. Shakespeare and Company in Paris is also a favourite [see page 112]. I remember once going to a small independent bookshop in the middle of America that had chickens running around it, and rodents nesting and racing around under glass floorboards. [This is Wild Rumpus Books: see page 217.]

There are some great independent children's bookshops in the UK, too – in Norfolk there's the Children's Book Centre, run by Marilyn Brocklehurst, and in Newcastle we've got the Seven Stories children's bookshop, which is excellent. Then there's the Children's Bookshop in Muswell Hill, which is always full of people, and helps dispel the myth that children aren't reading anymore. You go in to these bookshops and you can see a real energy around children and books.

You see, that's what good bookshops do: they work against the grain. They don't accept the pessimism, and they carry on with what they believe in. As Foyles do, as Seven Stories do, as Cogito Books do. They are a cultural force. I think generally there has been a bit of a turnaround in people's attitudes towards books. A few years ago there was a sense of doom, that it was all coming to an end, and some publishers seemed to believe it. Now there are some very powerful small independent presses, and some very powerful small independent bookshops, and I have high hopes for the future. Publishers are getting back to publishing lovely editions, and putting big efforts into making the books they produce look and feel fantastic. A good bookshop is not just about selling books from shelves, but reaching out into the world and making a difference. People never lose the sense of bookshop as a place where you can discover something. You can't browse online in the same way you browse in a really good bookshop, where you can always find something you want.

If I could open my own bookshop, I think I'd open a place a bit like Ultima Thule. I'd open it in Newcastle. It wouldn't be huge, and it would be tucked away somewhere quiet, but lots of people would know where it was. It would stock lots of really archaic stuff: small presses, aspiring poets, as well as loads of well-known books. We'd have lots of translated books in, and shelves and shelves of illustrated texts – because I love the process of matching words to art. It would be like a really good children's bookshop, in the sense that it would contain lots of different books, in different forms – but my bookshop wouldn't just be for children. It would be for everybody: a place to show what's really possible in the world of books today. **"**

❖

BOOKISH FACT

In earlier times, the maiming of authors
was a not uncommon practice. In the sixteenth century, critics would often cut off
the nose, the ears or the hands of authors
whose books they felt were too outspoken.
Following the Thirty Years' War in the
seventeenth century, Theodore Reinking
wrote a book whose anti-Swedish senti-
ments caused such outrage in the country
that he was thrown in jail and given an
ultimatum: eat your words, literally, or
we'll cut off your head. Theodore was
smart and decided to eat his own words.
He turned his book into a paste, and drank
the whole thing.

✶ ✶ ✶ SOME WONDERFUL THINGS ✶ ✶ ✶

◆ Salts Mill in West Yorkshire was completed in 1853, when it was the largest building in the world by total floor area. In 1987 its interior was renovated and split into sections that now include a bookshop and an art gallery. Salts Mill is the only gallery in the UK with a permanent David Hockney collection.

◆ Seven Stories in Newcastle is the only place in the UK dedicated to the art of children's books. Set in a converted warehouse, it has seven floors restored to house galleries, performance and creative spaces, a children's bookshop and a café. Over half a million people have visited since it opened in 2005, and a further 800,000 have visited its touring exhibitions around the UK. It works with children's charities to reach out to vulnerable children, introducing them to stories and illustrations, and helping them to express themselves creatively.

◆ SilverDell Bookshop in Kirkham is also an ice cream parlour. Its owner, Elaine Silverwood, makes the ice cream on site using Ayrshire cream and milk, as well as high-quality ingredients imported from Italy. Whenever they have an event with an author, Elaine creates a signature ice cream and names it after them. She made one for Sir Alex Ferguson with toffee ice cream, honeycomb, edible gold balls, red stars and chocolate footballs.

◆ The first customer to enter Storytellers Inc. in Lancashire was an eighty-year-old former teacher called Horace, who bought *Elmer the Elephant* to take back to his old school.

His friend filmed the purchase, because he apparently filmed everything that Horace did on his trips, making for a memorable sale. And from the oldest customer to the youngest: owner Katie Clapham says that, excluding bumps, they once sold a book to a three-day-old baby.

◆ Cogito Books in Hexham sponsors its local choir, who in turn visit at Christmas to fill the bookshop with carols. It also has *Where's Wally?* and Roald Dahl fancy-dress parties. 'The idea of a town without a bookshop is so sad,' says the owner, Claire, 'that I can't imagine not putting everything I have into running this place. We have the Cogito Reading Treat, where customers can come in to talk to me about books over tea and biscuits. I then come up with a bespoke reading list: six books hand-picked just for them.'

◆ Broadhursts Bookshop in Southport was opened in 1920 by Charles Broadhurst, a former president of the Antiquarian Booksellers Association. The shop is now run by Laurie Hardman. The restored building it's in dates back to 1875, when it was a house, and the main office is a gentlemen's room with an original fireplace, where there aren't only books but also old, royal letters including one from Alexandra, Queen of Yugoslavia.

◆

Book End, Bakewell, Peak District

Book End was opened by Ellie Potten and her mum in 2009. (They sold it at the end of last year, but it's still open, under new ownership.) It's a second-hand bookshop tucked inside an old stone building in the Peak District, next to a 700-year-old bridge, with chickens running about the place. Their first ever customer was a man called David, and every time he came in after that he was offered free tea and biscuits as a thank-you.

Ellie says she's one of those 'once a reader, always a reader' people. Growing up, she loved *Black Book*s and idolised Kathleen Kelly in Nora Ephron's rom-com *You've Got Mail*. Then she discovered Jeremy Mercer's *Books, Baguettes and Bedbugs*, about his year-long stay under the watchful eye of George Whitman at Paris's Shakespeare and Company, and the dream to own a bookshop became stronger. 'People thought we were mad,' says Ellie, 'when we mentioned our idea of opening a bookshop in the middle of a recession.'

'But the wonderful thing about ideas is how they can flourish at the right time, and in the right place. For me, my bookshop bloomed from one of the hardest times of my life. I started to develop agoraphobia when I was twenty, and when I realised that things were so bad that I couldn't leave the house any more, I made the difficult decision to leave university and move home. A year down the line, when I could still barely get out the front door, my mum Lynne took time off work to help get me back on my feet – and she soon realised that she didn't want to go back to her old job. It was at that point, with my confidence steadily improving, and both of us starting to look at entering work again, that the word "bookshop" first tumbled from our lips.

'It was in early 2009 that we started semi-seriously looking for properties and considering where we might like to open our still-not-quite-real bookshop. In the end we settled on the pretty little tourist town of Bakewell, the so-called Jewel of the Peak District, a fifteen-minute drive along the valley bottom from our house. While the rents for retail properties in the centre of town are quite steep, we found a little end shop, right by the famous 700-year-old bridge, for a much more reasonable figure that wouldn't blow our budget completely. It needed a lot of work doing to it inside, but actually it was lovely being in a slightly quieter, more picturesque spot, even if the footfall wasn't quite so high. It was particularly nice in summer, when the door was open and we could hear the ducks and geese nearby.

'The day we visited the shop with the agent and signed the lease was... surreal. No one imagines that dropping out of university and being rendered housebound could be the path to your dream job! Of course, we didn't have long to ponder this before the hard work started; within a day or two we'd launched into Project Renovation, roping in my grandparents and stepdad to help us overhaul the grubby ex-charity-shop interior as best we could. Doing everything on a shoestring was tricky, to say the least, but it's amazing how much a lick of sunshine paint and a new laminate floor brightened the place up!

'We knew there were already two big second-hand and antiquarian bookshops nearby, so rather than attempt to compete with their long-established vastness, we tried to stay true to what we were at heart – a small family-run bookshop catering for the locals, as well as the hordes of tourists who descended in the summer wanting holiday reads for their hotel rooms and bookish gifts to take home.

'Books aside, we were really just trying to create a nice atmosphere for people to come and browse. We'd stick little cards in books we'd enjoyed, and had a pinboard showcasing books we'd been reading, reviews and national bestseller lists. We had a cushion hanging on the wall for bottom-shelf browsing, a shop teddy called Aloysius reading in the children's section, and we sold eggs from our own hens by the dozen. In fact, some days the Orchard Girls were more popular than the books!

'My sister volunteered occasional days (her name badge read *HANNAH – Family Slave*) and she'd sit on the counter reading with a giant bag of pod peas. My grandmother could occasionally be spotted drifting through the shop with a mug of tea in one hand and a Mills and Boon novel in the other. We made firm friends with the owl man who displays by the bridge, the folks from the coffee shop opposite and the ladies in the boutique next door... and all the while customers would come and go.'

• A CHAT WITH CARYS BRAY •

Carys Bray's short story collection *Sweet Home* won Salt Publishing's Scott Prize. Her debut novel *A Song for Issy Bradley* is published by Hutchinson. Carys lives in Stockport with her husband and four children.

" I queued for two hours in the rain the first time I visited Broadhursts Bookshop in Southport. The staff had entered a national competition for the best Terry Pratchett window display, and their tableaux of Death (a skeleton borrowed from a local college) and The Luggage (a chest adorned with twelve dolls' legs bought on eBay), won the prize of a Terry Pratchett book signing. I read about the event in the local paper and, after school on a drizzly October evening, my children and I joined a queue that snaked down two streets.

When we finally shuffled into Broadhursts, wet and shivering, we stepped into another universe. The walls were wrapped in bookcases and glass-fronted cabinets. A book-packing station with a string dispenser and sheets of brown paper sat below an antique sign: PLEASANT BOOKS FOR THE CHILDREN. The air was warm with the grassy smell of paper and something else – an open fire. It felt as if we had been magicked into one of the shops in J.K. Rowling's Diagon Alley – I wouldn't have been surprised if a cousin of Mr Ollivander the wandmaker had emerged from behind a cabinet to whisper, 'The book chooses the child.'

The queue inched towards the foot of a green-spindled staircase, and as we edged upwards we passed framed vintage maps and illustrations from *Peter Pan*. We paused for a while on a small landing beside a cabinet full of copies of *Just William, Boy's Own* and *Rupert Annuals*, and then stepped round a corner and up a few more stairs where an open door was politely cordoned off by a purple, tasselled rope. The room behind the rope was furnished with a desk, an antique lamp and bookshelves stuffed with gold and red leather-jacketed tomes. A few more steps and we finally reached the cosy children's room. A large globe hung from the ceiling and beneath it, sitting behind a table, black fedora at his side, was Terry Pratchett, looking to all intents and purposes just like a wizard.

'Have I signed for you before?' he asked as I approached with the children.

'I don't think so,' I replied, because it suddenly seemed rude to say, 'No.'

He thought for a moment. 'Then I must have signed for your expression.'

And perhaps he had.

Afterwards, a local paper asked what he'd thought of Broadhursts. 'I can't actually believe it's real,' he said. 'I find it extremely hard to believe there are still bookshops like this.'

Looking back, I'm sure I wasn't the only person whose expression was an amalgamation of disbelief that such a place could exist, and delight at having made the discovery. **99**

❖

BOOKISH FACT

Part of the M6 toll road in the UK
is made out of pulped Mills and Boon
novels. A reported 2.5 million recycled
books were mixed in with asphalt and
tarmac to create the road surface.

◆

Linghams, Heswall, Wirral

Eleanor Davies and her husband Peter own Linghams bookshop in Heswall, which won the Independent Bookshop of the Year award in 2013. They've brought about three weddings as a result of staff members falling in love with fellow book-loving customers: the most recent, in 2013, was between Michael (their only male member of staff) and Joanne, whom he met at the Linghams Book Club. After the ceremony, they came to be photographed outside the shop and have confetti thrown over them by customers.

Eleanor told me about the bizarre things she's had to do as a bookseller. Once a customer came in and pushed a blank piece of paper and a pen under her nose: 'You sell music, don't you? Do you know the tune to "Happy Birthday"?'

Eleanor said she did, and asked if the customer would like her to hum the tune for her.

The customer shook her head. 'No, no. I want you to write it out here on this piece of paper.'

'The actual notes?'

'Yes, the actual notes. I want to ice them on my daughter's birthday cake!'

Eleanor dutifully wrote the score down. 'I bet they don't offer that kind of service in chain bookshops,' she added.

One of Eleanor's favourite bookshop events was with Rachel Joyce, the author of *The Unlikely Pilgrimage of Harold Fry*, a novel about a man called Harold who goes out one morning to post a letter and ends up walking from one end of the country to the other to try and save someone's life (see page 54). 'We always try to give a gift appropriate to each author who comes,' said Eleanor. 'With Rachel Joyce it was a shopping bag with a picture of the British Isles and Harold Fry's journey mapped out on it, but the route deviated to the Wirral so that he could stop at Linghams. The caption was "The More Likely Pilgrimage of Harold

Fry". The event itself was really special because people were so affected by Harold. One lady who came in to buy a ticket for it told me her husband had just read the book and as a result had rung up a brother he hadn't spoken to for fifteen years to make up a long-standing quarrel. It was the strong message of reconciliation in *Harold Fry* which had really spoken to him. I recounted this story to Rachel when she came to speak, and she was moved to tears.

'It is quite noticeable how often a customer comes in at a crucial moment in his or her life: this is frequently the time when people are seeking out books to help them through a crisis. So I have found myself speaking to people in the initial stages of bereavement, experiencing a marriage break-up or having great difficulties in child-rearing; people with severe health issues, and those with psychological and social problems. Bookshops are places where people congregate. Some of the people who pass through our doors do so on an almost daily basis, because they have found a warm and empathetic reception and a place where they can bring their troubles. For them, bookshops are safe places.'

◆

Scarthin Books, Cromford, Peak District

Scarthin Books calls itself a bookshop for 'the majority of minorities.' Owned by David Mitchell, the shop stocks both new and old books, and has gone from having one room and no staff to twelve rooms, a warehouse and seven full-time employees. Having been open for nearly forty years, they playfully say that their success is down to 'committed staff, organic growth, incompetence and homeliness', and that their main weakness is that 'once we were all about thirty; now we're mostly fifty-plus, fighting off early-retirement-envy and cancer.'

David says he based the layout of his bookshop on memories of weekly visits to 'the branching book-rich labyrinth of the Northamptonshire County Library.' This enables his staff to hide discount vouchers in amongst its shelves. Written along a high beam, for example, is 'The Utterly Unfair Tall Father Book Prize': '*If your father's head touches this beam (no platform or tiptoes!), claim £3-worth of bookshop credit!*' David's favourite room is the children's room: 'It was given a remarkable transformation eighteen months ago by two local installation artists, Katy and Claire. After having new shelves installed, I invited the two of them to come and spend the evening (and night) in the bookshop, with the briefest of briefs: to add a touch of magic to the room. After plying them with pizza and wine, I left them working throughout the night, returning at 8.30 a.m. the following morning to assess the results. What I walked into was beautiful. Above me was an inverted pop-up picture book, which they had created by pasting pages from broken books all over the ceiling. The lighting had been covered with drapes of fabric with hand-written messages from local school children, and a host of paper sculptures adorned every nook, cranny and corner.'

My favourite Scarthin Books story is that of a friendly book vandal. The bookshop had a title in stock called *Songs of Wild Birds*, published in 1941. The inscription inside, dated 1944, read: '*When this book is opened, birds begin to sing.*' In 2010, someone bought the book. A few days later the general manager, David Booker, found *Songs of Wild Birds* sitting on the shelf again. Puzzled, as he knew it had been sold, he opened the book and was surprised to find that it made a noise. It turned out that the customer had taken it home and installed a secret audio device inside, so that the pages, when turned, emitted different bird songs. The customer had then snuck the book back on the shelves for it to be re-discovered. Under the 1944 inscription '*When this book is opened, birds begin to sing*', they had added: '*They do now...*'

◆

Books & Ink, Banbury

Sam Barnes opened Books & Ink in Oxfordshire on Halloween in 2005 with her friend Sheryl. It sells both new and old books, and clearly there's something in the air when it comes to love and bookshops, because Sam met her boyfriend there, who was originally just a customer. It's clear that she loves what she does: the bookcases in the shop are hand-made and, when she first opened, she did a course in book-binding at Oxford Brookes so that she'd be able to do minor book repairs. When I visited, she and her mum immediately plied me with cups of tea and ginger biscuits and showed me their selection of old children's books. Inside an early twentieth-century schoolgirl story, in the very neat, cursive script of a young girl is one Sam's favourite inscriptions:

> *This book is the property of Annie Jeffrey.*
> *If this be borrowed by a friend, quite welcome shall he be to read, to*
> *study, to not lend but to return to me.*
> *Not that imparted knowledge doth diminish learning,*
> *but books I find often lent return to me no more.*
> *Read, understand what you read, and return in due time*
> <u>*with the corners of the leaves not turned down.*</u>

Like Eleanor at Linghams, Sam's bookshop has been able to help those going through difficult times. One customer had a friend who was very ill, and desperate to read *Heidi* one more time. He'd come across an abridged copy, and a new version, but neither was quite right, so Sam looked through everything she had and managed to unearth an old Puffin edition. It happened to be the exact copy his friend used to have.

• A CHAT WITH CAROLINE SMAILES •

Caroline Smailes lives in the north-west of England with her husband and three children. Her latest publication, *The Drowning of Arthur Braxton*, is her fifth novel.

" My imaginary bookshop would be a lighthouse – but not a lighthouse by the sea or on rocks. My bookshop would be a lighthouse in the middle of a town. It would look wonky, some would tut at it, others would whisper that it's an eyesore. On the top floor there would be something different. There would be disco balls, a roller-rink and power ballads from the 1980s available in headsets (free of charge). Not everyone would want to step inside.

Below that, I'd have all the delicious books muddled together on shelves that curved around the walls. My bookshop would be about searching, about climbing spiral staircases to stumble on a gem, about taking the time to discover a new book. The books would be dusty and wanting to be taken home. There wouldn't be a display table; I'd want all the books to be equal.

My bookshop would be a safe place; an escape from the real world. There would be curves to hide in, as not everyone likes to be seen. It would be open when it was both dark and light, and there would be free cake, too – far too much cake… 🙮

Almost daily, customers ask why I have a bookshop on a boat.
Sometimes their tone of voice suggests genuine interest.
Usually it is to precede a pun they actually believe to be
original – about it being a 'novel' idea. Or one 'hull' of an idea.
Or, when the Americans are in, a 'swell' idea. Once it was
asked with an inflection towards hysteria as the woman,
peering from a far window, shrieked: 'We're actually on water!
Maggie, why didn't you tell me this was a real boat!
You, at the desk, WHY IS THIS SHOP AFLOAT?' She then
paused, pulled a paperback to her chest as if to shield against
some kind of half-understood canal alchemy, before
reconsidering: 'But is it afloat? I just realised, this is all
probably some 3D illusion.' More thought. 'On stilts.'

from *The Bookshop That Floated Away* by Sarah Henshaw

◆

The Book Barge, Lichfield

For some reason, I've always wanted to own a houseboat. I'm not sure why, though perhaps the children's television show *Rosie and Jim* is to blame. Anyway, what could be better than a houseboat that is actually...a bookshop! Yes! Books on a boat, floating casually down a canal, where there's tea and biscuits and perhaps a sneaky glass of wine, too. If it's Saturday morning, there's sometimes even breakfast.

Let me explain. The Book Barge, moored mainly in Lichfield, is a 60-foot narrowboat converted into a bookshop, and is run by the majestic Sarah Henshaw. There are sofas to sit on, and refreshments to be had; there are typewriters artfully strewn around the place, and handmade book tokens hidden in amongst the shelves. Sarah has put her everything into making the Book Barge work; she's even living on it at the moment so that she can invest in its future. But I'm getting ahead of myself.

The Book Barge's original boat name is *Joseph*, and Sarah bought him in 2009. She also bought a rowing boat to keep *Joseph* company. (Her name is *Josephine*.) There's even a bookshop rabbit on board, by the name of Napoleon Bunnyparte. (Sometimes he eats the books.)

It's been a busy five years. When Sarah first had the idea for the bookshop, she approached banks asking for start-up loans. Trying to be original, she presented her business plan to them in the form of a book, complete with fake reviews and pictures from *The Wind in the Willows* to show how wonderful the bookshop would be once it was up and running. She even included illustrations of Cleopatra's barge (from Shakespeare's *Antony and Cleopatra*):

> The barge she sat in, like a burnished throne,
> Burned on the water: the poop was beaten gold;
> Purple the sails, and so perfumèd, that
> The winds were lovesick with them.

The Book Barge was going to be amazing, the business plan declared; it was going to be the stuff of legend. Sarah smiled her sweetest smile. 'Help us do this!' The banks raised their eyebrows, sighed, and said no.

So, plan B. With financial help from her family, the Book Barge was bought, gutted, refurbished and opened in 2009, and initially business was good. People hailed the shop as 'magical,' and it made it on to many 'Top Ten Best Bookshops of the World' lists. However, it's all very well being called 'magical', but if that doesn't translate into sales, then book-sellers don't magically get to eat. It wasn't easy; there was a recession and the world of bookselling was changing. The question everyone started asking Sarah was not, 'Why do you have a bookshop on a boat?' but 'Why do you have a bookshop at all?'

Keen to show that bookshops weren't (and aren't) a dying breed, and taking advantage of the fact that if you have a bookshop on a boat you don't have to sell books in the same place all the time, Sarah decided to set off on a six-month journey travelling around the canals of Britain. The Book Barge didn't have a shower, a kitchen or a loo, so her plan was to use Facebook and Twitter to announce her location and request food, shelter and bathroom facilities in exchange for books. Her rea-soning was that if books could be bartered for services, then it would show that those books were actually *worth* something, and prove that people still found them of value.

It was a brave move. She set off on her own in May 2011, never having mastered canal locks, and threw herself at the mercy of book-lovers who lived nearby wherever she happened to be docking that night. It was a massive act of trust, giving out mobile numbers to strangers, and accepting food from people she didn't know. There were only a couple of odd people along the way, and one of those was in Australia. He sent her an email suggesting that Sarah change course and sail across the world to visit his country instead. He even plotted out a route for her, saying she should holiday in Asia along the way. She politely declined. Over the course of six months, Sarah travelled more than a thousand miles, adopted a pigeon, was robbed, made it into the national newspapers, and was even thrown out of Bristol. You can read all about her adventures in her delightful and hilarious book *The Bookshop That Floated Away*.

The Book Barge actually features in *Weird Things Customers Say in Bookshops*, with a selection of its own 'Weird Things.' As you can imagine, a floating bookshop can attract some odd questions. When I was last there (in the days before Sarah lived on the boat, when it was clearly just a bookshop), a woman spent a good half-hour sitting on the sofa, reading a book she'd picked up. Then she turned to Sarah and said, 'I must say, I think it's lovely that you invite people into your house like this.' She was quite startled when we explained that this wasn't a house, but actually a bookshop, though why the woman was more comfortable with the idea of casually wandering into someone's home, I don't know. I think my favourite customer, however, was a man who came in and whispered, 'I know I look like Saddam Hussein, but don't worry, I'm not him.'

There are many events aboard the Book Barge: letterpress workshops, a very successful book club, and an occasional breakfast club, for which you can book a slot on a Saturday morning: Sarah will make you breakfast, and you can read books whilst cruising down the canal. The breakfast club was made possible because Sarah's boyfriend, Stu, a carpenter, helped her install 'reading pods' for children to sit in, as well as a loo and a small kitchen.

The make-over was pretty essential, as Sarah is now planning her next great adventure. Whilst browsing online, she spied a plot of land for sale along the Canal du Nivernais, in Burgundy, with an unconverted barn and a well for €19,000. She'd always dreamed of taking the Book Barge to France. (One day she hopes to take it all the way to the Black Sea.) She showed the listing to Stu, and they both hurried across to France to take a look. 'When we got there and saw it,' says Sarah, 'and imagined all the work that would have to be done to make it liveable, and the long wrangles for permission to moor the boat, and the bats living inside the barn, and the birds nesting alongside them, we paused awhile. Then we considered the fact we can't speak much French, that the market for English books in a hamlet of no more than thirty houses is limited, to say the least, and that waiting for a calm enough day to chug the boat over to Calais could be a long while. And then we just grinned and grinned and bought it anyway. Because we're idiots, mainly. But also because, at just that moment, the strains of violins began to carry on the breeze from the big house across the water, and for a minute or two it felt like the future could be both glorious and strange.'

To save money to afford the move, Sarah and Stu are living on the Book Barge for a year. They've joined a local gym so they can use the showers there, and Sarah's working full-time as a school librarian, as well as running the shop in the evenings and the weekends, and sleeping in the boat in the middle of a busy marina with people peering through the curtains, now even more perplexed about whether the boat is a bookshop or a house. If that isn't dedicated bookselling, I don't know what is.

❖

Bookish Fact

In Shakespeare's day, decomposed bodies were often dug up and burned, to make room for the newly dead. The Bard despised this practice, and so wrote a curse to go on his headstone that damns anyone trying to move his body:

Good friend for Jesus' sake forbear,
To dig the dust enclosed here.
Blessed be the man that spares these stones,
And cursed be he that moves my bones.

◆

The Yellow-Lighted Bookshop, Tetbury and Nailsworth

Hereward Corbett runs two branches of his bookshop in Gloucestershire, and also set up the Yellow-Lighted Book Festival. 'The name of our shop comes from the title of a brilliant book by an American called Lewis Buzbee,' says Hereward.

'Lewis got the title of the book from a letter that Vincent van Gogh – a one-time bookseller himself – wrote to his brother, wishing that he could go back to Paris and, on a wet November evening, paint 'a bookshop... with the shop window yellow-pink... and the passers-by black.'

'All this gave us something to live up to as a bookshop. Six years on, and a second bookshop opened, we try to be ethical – we only use green power, for example – stock great books, and be gentle and kind and thoughtful in what we do. If we make an impact, we want it to be a positive one. Thankfully, the other people who work here are rather better at all this than I am. We are hugely lucky to be here. Someone once described me as a "civilised hustler". If I can be a successful and ethical one too – by selling books – that's an achievement.'

◆

George Bayntun, Bath

Bath is one of my favourite cities. The buildings are beautiful, you can go for walks along the canal and dream of living in a houseboat, and of course there are the Roman Baths: sacred thermal springs, with a legend surrounding them that the water saved ancient King Bladud and his herd of pigs from leprosy. King Bladud is rumoured to have created the springs using magic some 2500 years ago.

George Bayntun bookshop is near the railway station, so always my first port of call. You can't just walk in, though: you need to ring the doorbell and wait. While I wait, I imagine I'm being assessed to see if I have enough love for books to be let in, which makes entering even more magical.

What I love most about the bookshop is the way it's set up. You've knocked, you've been let in and now you can roam the expanse of leather and gilt. There are bookcases under the stairs and children's books fill the basement. It's like an overgrown doll's house. You can browse completely undisturbed, disappear behind the bookshelves, and lose an hour or two. The bookshop's famous bindery has been open since the 1800s, and even now there are eleven binders working there, with clients across the globe. Between them they've been in the field for 337 years. The bindery also claims to have the largest collection of hand tools and blocks in the world – over 15,000 – some of which date back to the eighteenth century. The bookshop also received the patronage of Queen Mary in 1950, when she granted George Bayntun the appointment of Bookseller to Her Majesty.

◆

Mr. B's Emporium of Reading Delights, Bath

Nic Bottomley and his wife Juliette were lawyers in London and Prague. On their honeymoon, they talked about what they wanted to do in the future and, both being book-lovers, both a little sick of law, they decided to quit their jobs and move back to the UK to open a bookshop.

Nic wanted to make sure they did things properly, so he hopped in his car and travelled around the north of England and south of Scotland for a month, visiting as many independent bookshops as possible, to collect sound advice on how to run a bookshop well. Independents, I've found, are very willing to help new starters succeed by sharing the details of their successes – and failures. Nic and Juliette were helped out by her brother Harvey and, less helpfully, by their Czech bookshop dog, Vlashka. Mr B's opened in 2006.

'We've learned everything on our feet,' says Nic. 'I mean, on the day we opened we weren't sure how to use the till. We've grown through our experiences: we've changed our shop by adding another floor; we've learned you can make a bookseller out of a book-lover who's really good with people;

we've learned about making interesting displays tailored to where we are – for instance we converted a claw-foot bath into a book display table, and we run reading spas where customers can come to our Bibliotherapy Room for a one on one chat to come up with a reading list suited specifically for them. We do some limited editions of books, too, working alongside publishers: it's all about offering unique experiences.'

Wanting to create different kinds of bookshop events, Nic called on three musician friends, who formed the Bookshop Band . They compose songs about books written by the authors they do events with. It's really taken off, and they've toured Britain. The band has written over a hundred songs, and Nic's favourites include 'How Not to Woo a Woman', which is based on *The Unlikely Pilgrimage of Harold Fry*. You can listen to their songs on their website, thebookshopband.co.uk.

• A CHAT WITH RACHEL JOYCE •

Rachel Joyce is the author of the international bestseller *The Unlikely Pilgrimage of Harold Fry*. Her second novel, *Perfect*, was published in 2013 to critical acclaim. She has also written for radio and television, including over twenty original afternoon plays for BBC Radio 4.

> " When I was really little, I loved *My Naughty Little Sister*, and anything with rhymes – as children do. We had many books in our house, but we went to the library a lot, too. We didn't go to bookshops in the same way that I take my children now.

I don't have a specific favourite when it comes to bookshops, because they all have something different going on. I love a bookshop where there is light and enough space to take in the books. There is a wonderful bookshop in Toronto with a huge glass chandelier that hangs over the shop as if it's a ballroom. You feel something special is going to happen the moment you walk in. Bath is blessed with two stunning bookshops. There is

Topping's with its polished wood floors and exquisitely wrapped first editions. I sort of hum when I open the door. And then, only down the road, there is Mr. B's Emporium of Reading Delights, another chandelier bookshop, with the Bookshop Band. It's a very moving thing when somebody takes your book and makes something else out of it – a gift, actually. I remember when I first heard their Harold Fry song – it made me cry. I haven't heard anyone else do anything quite like that – sing about a book.

My children are so used to being able to buy things on computers, but there is nothing like going into a bookshop and picking up a book and being able to examine the style of it before jumping in and deciding to have it. I can never go into a bookshop and leave empty handed.

It's a sort of ritual, really, the journey you go on with a book in a bookshop. It starts with your eye being drawn to a title or an image, and you pick that book up and read the back of it, and then you choose to look inside. There you stand, with this real thing in your hand that you can hold and weigh and even smell, perhaps, before you begin looking at the fonts used and the way the pages are put together. We don't do this enough: go into bookshops and touch the books. We should choose them in the same way we choose friends. I want my children to understand this and treasure them.

I also love it when booksellers have shelves of recommendations with handwritten reviews, or when a bookseller comes up to you in a bookshop and starts chatting to you, and then recommends something. I've met wonderful booksellers all over the world, but one woman in particular stands out for me. She worked for a big chain bookstore in Toronto, where each bookseller had a quota of books that they had to sell. She had decided that she was going to channel all of her energy into hand-selling 400 copies of *The Unlikely Pilgrimage of Harold Fry*. She considered it her project, and she focused on men who had dismissed the book initially, simply because a woman had written it.

And if I had to open a bookshop of my own? Well, it probably wouldn't make any money. So I am no help to anyone. But I would set it somewhere with a garden, where light poured in through the windows. Sit in the sun, I'd tell my customers. Open this book. Try it. It won't do any harm, after all, to sit a while and read. **"**

◆

Harris & Harris Bookshop, Clare, Suffolk

Harris & Harris have this written across one wall of their bookshop:

'Never lend books, for no-one ever returns them. The only books I have in my library are books that other people have lent me.'

Anatole France.

Very wise.

A customer once told Kate Harris, the owner, that walking around her bookshop was like walking around Kate's mind, because the curation of the place was so *her*. This is, I think, what all good bookshops should be like: the tangible, bookish expression of the people who own them.

Kate had worked in other people's bookshops, including Much Ado (see below), but says that hers came about quite by accident:

'It was only about five months after we moved to Suffolk. My father had not long passed away, and my mother had come to visit us for the day. As we drove into Clare, we parked up in the only space left, in front of one of the antique shops. As we got out of the car, my eye caught a large Staffordshire figure of William Shakespeare in the antique shop. We went in to get a closer look. The shop owner just happened to hear my mother say that if she bought it for me, I would have to open a bookshop, because that's where such a thing should live. He told me that the owner of one of the gift shops on the high street was about to move, and that they might be looking for someone to fill her old shop.

'So, with William Shakespeare bought, and tucked under my arm, I positively ran to the gift shop. Alas, she had someone lined up to move in... But that fell through, and a phone call a few days later led to a meeting – and the deal was done! I opened about three months later. All from an overheard conversation, and with the help of William Shakespeare!'

◆

Much Ado, Alfriston, Sussex

Much Ado in Alfriston has bookcases with second-hand books outside, new books inside, and antiquarian books on the floor above. It's owned by Cate Olson and Nash Robbins.

Cate grew up on a farm in an Amish community in Pennsylvania. 'I always wanted to sell books,' she says. 'I used to sit under my grandfather's desk, pull the books off the lower shelf, and try to sell them back to him. He said that he knew I was never going to be a librarian with an attitude like that!

'I was also obsessed with England when I was a child. Whenever I had my allowance, I would make people translate what it would be in pounds – just in case I was magically transported there. That way, I'd know how much money I had to spend in my pocket. England seemed very exotic to me.'

Cate opened her first bookshop in New England, which is where she met Nash. He was working as a reporter for the local paper at the time, and brought in a box of books to sell. He didn't leave, and says he never looked back. 'We had three different premises in America,' he says, 'all within about a hundred yards of each other.

'We just kept expanding. One of the things that, I think, made us very successful was the fact that we were anglophiles. We came over to England to buy books, and shipped them back. We just liked the look and feel of some of the English editions more, and quite a few of them hadn't filtered across to the States at all, so we were selling books that weren't available anywhere else.'

Cate and Nash ended up staying for longer and longer periods of time when they came to the UK, and eventually bought a cottage, which they'd rent out when they went back to the States. 'Every time we came over, we'd spend our days buying books for the shop from second-hand bookshops,' says Cate. 'Our treat at the end of each day was to find a new independent bookshop and buy books for ourselves. Over the years, we found that there were less and less of those bookshops for us to go to.'

So, having run Much Ado in America for twenty years, in 2003 Cate finally decided to transport herself and Nash permanently to the UK, and bring their bookshop with them. Much Ado is now in Sussex, and it's Bill Bryson's favourite bookshop (see page 199). Their home is next door to the shop, and between the two is their garden, and a courtyard where their three bantam hens happily run around. In 2013, they set up the Friends of Much Ado, which customers can join for £100 a year (they have 116 members already). With this, amongst other things such as free reading consultations, members get access to the Friends' Suite, which Cate and Nash call 'book-lined rooms for browsing, reading and dreaming.' It's a private section of the shop on the first floor, filled with beautiful antiquarian books and writing tables. Alongside the shop, they run Prospero's Project, which each year raises money for a literacy charity. In 2013, they became Santa's elves and sewed and decorated hundreds of Christmas stockings which they sold in their bookshop, raising £2,300 for Kids' Company.

❖

Bookish Fact

Lord Byron loved dogs. When he
became a Cambridge scholar, he was
appalled to discover that the university
did not permit students to keep dogs
in their dorms. So, he rebelled and
decided to keep a pet bear called Bruin
instead. As there were no rules in the
college handbook stating that bears
were not allowed, Cambridge had no
legal grounds to complain. Byron
even joked that he might get Bruin
to apply for a college fellowship.

• A CHAT WITH ALI SMITH •

Ali Smith was born in Inverness in 1962 and now lives in Cambridge. Her first book, *Free Love*, won the Saltire First Book Award, and she has since been shortlisted for both the Orange Prize and the Man Booker Prize (twice). Her most recent publications are *There but for the*, *Artful* and *Shire*.

" It was probably my mother who made me fall in love with stories.

She didn't really read to me, and neither did my father. I had four older siblings, so they were a bit exhausted with all of that by the time I came along. On Saturday night, though, it was bath time. That was the evening that the immersion heater was put on – you know, those were the days before central heating – and, after the bath, my mother would sit me on her knee and she would turn into different characters and regale me with their life stories. I remember being absolutely terrified by some of those characters. There would be some she'd share with my siblings, but a few were reserved just for me. My mum was Irish, but we grew up in the north of Scotland, and one of the characters was this very northern Scottish character – a woman she'd made up – from the Outer Hebrides, a character who was very hard-done-by, and her name was Morag. What Morag did was complain all the time, but in a really rich and at the same time totally mundane way, so if my mum was being Morag I was listening to what was, essentially, an improvised litany, a prose poem. I loved that time with my mum; it was a real generosity on her part because she didn't have much time.

When I was little, my mother wasn't keen on me using the public library – she'd had four kids' worth of library fines to pay for the twelve years before I was born. But the house was full of books belonging to my sisters and brothers anyway, mainly school books, and the Scottish curriculum when I was a kid was pretty fantastic; the cupboard above my head was full of really great books. So, when I was eight, nine, ten I was reading Orwell and Joyce, and I didn't realise until later that that's what they were.

There was a bookshop in Inverness called Melvens, and the kind of books they sold were Scottish tourism books – Loch Ness Monster, Mary Queen of Scots, that kind of thing, mainly. But when I was about fifteen, they opened a downstairs department where they sold the new Penguins and Faber and Picador paperbacks; I think the first thing I discovered was Simone de Beauvoir, then all manner of other writers. When you went down there, you'd always meet amazing people who loved books, too. It was an adventure.

At the same time, a little second-hand independent bookshop opened and I spent a lot of my time there. It was called Leakey's, and the books there were old Penguins – John Wyndhams, Doris Lessings, Thomas Manns ... I bought Sophocles there, too, and Epicurus and Tennessee Williams. I'd come home with such an eclectic mix of stuff. Every weekend I'd go there after I'd done my Saturday job at Littlewoods. I worked in the café, used to get paid £10 for the day, and at lunchtime we'd pick up our pay packet and I'd go and spend it all in the local record shop, or at the bookshop, or a mixture of both.

I started writing when I was about seven, partly because we were asked to write a series of poems at school, which I made into a small book. I wasn't asked to do that; I just enjoyed writing them so much. There was also a book I read at that time called *Ginger Over the Wall*, about a group of boys who kicked a ball over their garden wall into an old lady's house, and then became friends with her. I remember feeling that it was unfair that there were no girls in it, so I rewrote it for girls.

There's a certain thrill of seeing your first book in a shop, I suppose. I first saw *Free Love and Other Stories* in Waterstones in

Cambridge. I also saw a copy of it in a bookshop in Boston in the US, and I was completely amazed by how far its print run had stretched. But that's nothing to the real thrill of being in a brilliant bookshop which you can't leave without all the books you feel you have to take home with you, books you can't leave that shop without.

Second-hand bookshops in Cambridge, where I live, seem to get all manner of interesting stock, especially from university scholars studying obscure things. I love the cycle of that: the books come in, and then go out again into the city. I love a book that's done a bit of travelling. One of my favourite discoveries from a second-hand bookshop was a copy of D.H. Lawrence's *Birds, Beasts and Flowers*. It's got a yellow cover, 1930s, and it's inscribed to 'F. N. LW from P. A. – Sept 1933.' There's a photo stuck inside it, of a woman in a bathing suit doing what looks like her make-up, looking into a little mirror, by the river in Grantchester. The book, being Lawrence, is full of really sensual, full-on and argumentative love poems. But towards the very back of the book some of the pages haven't been cut. So, was it just tiredness at Lawrence, or did something happen in their relationship, to stop the person reading? I'd love to know, but I know I never will. All books hold a history. I love second-hand books for that fact: you just hold them in your hand and they're full of story, apart from what's written inside them.

There's something magical about bookshops, too. Especially now, when chain bookshops often can't afford to stock really eclectic stuff and take as many risks as they used to, independents have stepped forward and shown that they are willing to do just that. The new independent eye is an eye for things that are really exciting, current, and also for things which are hidden just under the radar. You know a good bookshop because you can't just walk past it. Bookshops mean a kind of sanity, and a communal individualism. That's how I see it; a good bookshop will cater for all of our tastes individually and have an eye to all of us at the same time. A bookshop is a bookshop owner's vision, and book-lovers tend to share visions. At the end of the day, it doesn't matter so much what publishers declare to be the latest trend, or what's going to win such-and-such an award that year. A bookshop's aim is the same as a reader's aim, and it isn't restricted to time: they help things stay steady, and balance everything out. All they want, all we want, is a good book.

If I opened my own bookshop? I remember when I first found a copy of Tove Jansson's *The Summer Book*, a slim Penguin from the 1970s – you wouldn't even notice it on a shelf. My bookshop would be full of those types of things: the books that, when you picked them up, you knew immediately that that was the book you were going to read that day. Moreover: whatever you'd been planning on doing, you'd just sit down with that book you'd picked up by chance, and read that instead. The days when we sit down with a book so good we don't get up until it's read – those are some of the best days of our lives. **"**

❖

Bookish Fact

Charles Dickens was extremely interested in the paranormal. He was one of the earliest members of the Ghost Club, the oldest organisation in the world dedicated to psychic research.

◆

The Haunted Bookshop, Cambridge

The Haunted Bookshop is tucked down a side street in Cambridge. Its owner, Sarah Key, has been selling books since 1987, and jokes that the books are what's holding up the shop. It's on two floors, and sells antiquarian books, specialising in children's literature, though you never know what someone's going to come in and sell, and in one box of books she once found a seventeenth-century book on angling.

I'd assumed the bookshop was named after Christopher Morley's book of the same name: a novel about the ghosts of all great literature haunting libraries and bookshops, but Sarah has another story:

'It was called the Haunted Bookshop when I bought it in the 1990s, for a variety of reasons, but David, the previous owner, did say that the bookshop was haunted. He reckoned there was a very grumpy gentleman in the cellar, and a lady who hovered around the stairs. David actually called me two weeks before he died to tell me that if there was a way to come back and haunt the bookshop himself, then he would. On the day he died, the books went a little crazy, and there was a lot of movement on the shelves – so make of that what you will!'

◆

The Madhatter Bookshop, Burford, Oxfordshire

The Madhatter Bookshop in the Cotswolds is half bookshop, half hat shop. The owner, Sara's, great-grandmother was a milliner in Manchester, and when her local bookshop went up for sale Sara wanted to take it over, but thought she should pair books with something else to reach a wider market. '*You* should sell hats, too!' said one of her teenage daughters.

'When the hats arrive in the shop, it's just like Christmas,' says Sara. 'And I've been pleasantly surprised by the cross-over of purchases: people who come in to buy a hat often leave with a book too, and vice versa.'

Oxfordshire is the home of Lewis Carroll, and Sara's planning on having many an *Alice in Wonderland* themed tea party in the future. After all, you can have unbirthday parties three hundred and sixty-four days of the year!

◆

Blackwell's, Oxford

Blackwell's on Broad Street was opened in 1879 by Benjamin Henry Blackwell, the son of a librarian. His own son Basil was the first in the family to go to university, and joined the bookshop in 1913, after working for a London publisher. Basil brought his knowledge of the publishing trade back with him, and helped build up Blackwell's own printing house, which kick-started the careers of many popular writers. They published J. R. R. Tolkien's first poem 'Goblin Feet' in a collection of Oxford poetry in 1915. Tolkien had a balance outstanding on his account with Blackwell's, so instead of paying him for the piece, Blackwell's cancelled his debt instead.

The Oxford bookshop was the only branch of Blackwell's for over a hundred years, all the way up until the 1990s when they decided to expand into a chain. They're still owned by the Blackwell family, but now have over forty branches across the UK, plus pop-up shops, and each branch is managed autonomously. Their flagship store in Oxford was originally only twelve feet square, but now it hosts four whole floors of bookshelves, and a separate art and poster shop, too. The main building stretches from the top floor, where second-hand books are sold, all the way down to the vast Norrington Room in the basement, which alone boasts three miles of shelving. When you stand in the middle of the room you can't easily see the other side, and it has a stage, too, constructed in 2011, where plays are sometimes performed in the evenings.

Legend has it that Oxford University's origins lie with a beautiful, pious princess called Frideswide. Frideswide wanted to become a nun, but the king wished to marry her, and to escape his pursuit of her she ran away to Oxford. The king followed, but when he reached the edge of the town he was struck blind. Only after begging for forgiveness and agreeing to give her her freedom was his sight magically restored. Frideswide was then free to build a nunnery on the site of what is now Christ Church cathedral, and the earliest colleges of the university were created around it as a place of learning for monastic scholars. Since then, Oxford's beautiful old buildings have definitely lent themselves to literature: the city is the location for *Alice in Wonderland* and *His Dark Materials*. Had Hitler conquered Britain, apparently he planned to use the city as the capital of his kingdom, which is one of the reasons why it was never bombed during the Second World War.

One evening in April 2012 I arrived in Oxford at the invitation of Blackwell's deputy manager Zool Verjee. I wasn't there to sell books: as well as writing *Weird Things Customers Say in Bookshops,* I'm a poet, and Zool's plan was for me to spend a day wandering around the bookshop, writing a poem for each floor. Blackwell's was just closing as I got there; the staff had just finished running the Oxford Literary Festival, organising 350 author events in just nine days. It made my head hurt just thinking about it. They are, in fact, pretty legendary when it comes to running events: besides the festival, which they call 'one event', they run another 250 throughout the year, and have a wonderful Author Signing Book full of messages from the writers they've hosted. My particular favourite is a hand-drawn Wild Thing left by Maurice Sendak in the 1980s. In the staff offices off the top floor, there's even a whole bookcase of novels, and non-fiction, dedicated to books that mention Blackwell's.

The following morning, having spent a very comfortable night in the bookshop flat across the road above their music shop (I'd have happily slept in the shop itself, hidden in amongst the books), I headed to their staff briefing at 9 a.m, before beginning to walk quietly around the bookshop itself, not looking for things to buy, but simply absorbing the feel of the place. 'I really feel like the books have souls, you know,' Euan Hirst, Oxford's Academic Manager, said to me. 'When I walk past the shelves, they stir, and whisper, "Why haven't you read me yet?"' He's quite right. The more I walked around, the more I felt as though the bookshop's silence was loaded: the books holding their breath, trying to keep their stories inside. Here are two extracts from the poems I wrote that day.

THE LOST WORLD
Second-hand and antiquarian section

First, we go back in time.
To those who have lost their homes –
torn their dust jackets on the way out, to those
who will know many people. They sit:

their leather whispers to remind us
of evacuees. Their outgrown name tags.
Please take us in.

They have been waiting
all their lives with broken backs.
One, brazen, face-out says:
'*We Ain't What We Ought to Be*'
and they nod. Held tight.

A solar system centred on
the alphabet.

They hold their breath for potential homes.
Smooth their dog ears out, and
at the very edge, Archaeology stands – proud
as though it were he
who unearthed the rest.

THE MAGICIAN'S BOOK
Fiction and children's section

...This is Lyra's Oxford
and if books had daemons
they'd whisper stories as well –
before and after the main one had finished.

They'd chatter fairy tales in our ears
before we're even born.

Euan, Zool and Rebecca MacAlister, the Branch Manager, often talk about 'the Blackwellian Family', which doesn't just include those by the name of Blackwell, but all of the staff who now work there. Over a cup of tea they told me why they love the shop so much.

'When I applied for the Manager job here, I was interviewed by Toby Blackwell himself,' said Rebecca. 'They dropped me off at his house and said 'See you in two hours' – I was so nervous! But he, more than anything or anyone, made me want to work here: he wouldn't let anyone else hire the manager of his flagship shop because he's still so passionate about the company. You feel like you're part of a family and, when I lock the door of the shop every night, I feel as though I'm repeating history. That's the romantic side of it all, and that's why we do it.'

'There's a feeling, I think, that we owe a debt to our history,' added Euan. 'Over the past hundred and forty years, the company has done pretty much everything, and it's an amazing guide for where we can go next. I'd be surprised if we're not printing books again in the next five years; we really want to take the shop's history full circle. We've got a phrase we use here: 'the cutting edge of tradition', and that's exactly how it is. We're embedded in the history of Oxford, but at the same time we were also the first bookshop to trade on the internet. It's all about a mixture of being innovative and recognising that we're guardians of a pretty important flame. We like to explore and develop, but we don't have algorithms here – we have booksellers. And we're incurably inquisitive.'

• A CHAT WITH BRIAN ALDISS •

Born in 1925, Brian Aldiss is best known for his science fiction novels and short stories. In 2000 he was named a Grand Master by the Science Fiction Writers of America, and he has received two Hugo Awards, one Nebula Award and one John W. Campbell Memorial Award. His books have recently been republished by the Friday Project.

" After the Second World War I left the army and went back to my home down in Devon. However, I found it all terribly boring. After all, I'd been to exciting places like Burma – so I got on a train to Oxford and, very sensibly, I've lived in Oxford ever since.

Naturally, I had to get a job, so I decided to apply to a local bookshop, Sanders of Oxford – an antiquarian bookshop that still trades today. Back then it was run by Frank Sanders who, curiously enough, had come from Barnstaple, too, and we got on very well together. I learned an enormous amount from Frank because he was a hoarder – in particular, a hoarder of precious books. He had a little locked room upstairs that contained all kinds of mysterious things, like *Ackerman's Oxford* and *Ackerman's Cambridge*. The Ackerman books were illustrated histories of the colleges – very beautiful, very dignified art. There was also a massive folio containing many Hogarth engravings, and of course there were the teeming books – so many, many books.

As a bookseller, I quickly fell in love with two opposing things: Thomas Hardy and his poems, and the Russians. I adored the Russian novels. And, actually, even down in Devon I had somehow acquired *The Diary of Marie Bashkirtseff*. That's not a very familiar name to everyone, but to me the book was revelatory. Marie Bashkirtseff came from a wealthy Russian family, and her parents had broken up: her father remained in Russia but her mother took her down to Nice to live in exile. This incredible journal of Marie's has been translated several times. I have never loved a book more. When I was eight I read it compulsively, and I still have it here on my shelves. From Bashkirtseff I found Dostoevsky, and then eventually Tolstoy. And now that I'm ancient, I only read Tolstoy, and I only read his novel *Resurrection*, because it contains so many elements of life. And so many elements of my life, too.

As for the bookshop, for me it was the curiosity of undiscovered books that was wonderful. Although I was a keen reader, the books that were being read by men in Oxford colleges were often ones I wasn't familiar with. It was a joy to read those. And then there were the customers. I admit we often made fun of them: there was an Oxford scholar who came in, and he'd written a book of poems which he was always talking about – on and on. Quite a bore. We had a lot of celebrated writers who came in, too. Some were very nice: John Masefield for instance. John Piper, the artist, was usually extremely arrogant towards the assistant. Evelyn Waugh was always pretty miserable. And on a Saturday evening, Dylan Thomas, in the days of his fame, would come in and chat to Frank Sanders. As we closed up, Frank and Dylan would walk up the street arm in arm and Dylan would say: 'Frank, you couldn't lend me ten quid, could you?', and Frank would cry 'Of course!' and rush back to the till. Then Dylan would thank him and disappear off into the night, and Frank would smack himself on the forehead and cry, 'Oh, no! I've done it again! What a fool I am!' That was the human comedy of working at Sanders.

Something which wasn't so fun was the salary. It was absolutely miserable. So after a while, I left. I'd been there about three or four years by that time, and I went instead to Parker's, which was a bookshop on Broad Street owned by Blackwell's, and there I would think about how strange the bookselling world of Oxford was. So I wrote a letter to the editor of the *Bookseller* – I didn't admit that I'd had nothing else published, probably a couple of short stories in print by then, but not much – and said I would like to do a comic page every week about it. They became 'The Brightfount Diaries', 'Brightfount' being a kind of play on 'Blackwell', and they were very popular. A couple of years later, the editor of Faber and Faber asked me if I'd like to make the columns into a book. I thought, 'Well, if the readers don't laugh, I needn't do it again!' But they did laugh, and my career as a writer took flight.

Nowadays I occasionally do a stint in London with my friend Timothy Ackroyd at a little bookshop called the Idler Academy, where we talk about books and writing. That's always fun. Moreover, I'm now good friends with the Bodleian Library who, on my death, are going to receive my journals, handwritten and illustrated. I'm now on volume seventy-eight, which is two and a half yards of bookshelf space. The Bodleian were also able to dig up the original two hardback copies of *The Adventures of Whip Donovan*, which was a book I wrote when I was fourteen. It's handwritten by me, and illustrated by me too, in watercolour. It's actually being printed as a facsimile by the Friday Project – isn't that fun?

If I could open my own bookshop, I'd open it in dear old Oxford. I owe so much to this place. When I was first submitting my short stories to various places in New York, my letter would always include my address, and that would always include 'Oxford.' Even people in New York knew where Oxford was, and I felt very proud to live in the city. If I could open a bookshop in Oxford, I think the commercial thing would be to include old and new books, and one would have to exercise careful judgement about the rest of the business. I mean, everything is changing now. Thankfully the bookselling industry goes on. My new publisher, the Friday Project, does very well, moving with the times. But are books going to die out? Many people have prophesied that, but I say that can't happen. Books are important, so very important. They teach you things; they show you different views of the world. You can't help having a soft spot for books, and everything that they stand for. **,,**

◆

P & G Wells, Winchester

P&G Wells is the oldest bookshop in the UK still trading. In fact, receipts have been found dating back to 1729, detailing the local college's purchases of a Latin grammar book (9d), paper (4d), an article book (3d) and an inkhorn (4d). Only half the bill was paid, which seems to have been common practice back then, and made it very difficult for retail businesses to stay afloat: almost everything was paid on account. The oldest bookshop in Europe is the Bertrand Bookstore in Portugal, which opened in 1732, and whilst P&G Wells' trading pre-dates this, it didn't actually move into these premises in College Street until the 1750s, so Portugal stay ahead.

Winchester goes back to Saxon times, when it used to be the capital of England, and its magnificent Gothic cathedral is one of the largest in Europe. Over the years P&G Wells has passed through many hands. Ambrose Hollaway is the first trader associated with it, and then in the late 1750s it was taken over by the Burdons who, as well as expanding the bookselling business, started to print textbooks for Winchester College. New owners Robbins and Wheeler printed the local newspaper and helped support the local library by setting up a new reading room: for a subscription you could donate books, or pay 4d per volume for the first twelve months. Robbins unfortunately went bankrupt when he opened a pub and brewery, and so the bookshop was taken over by a London bookseller, David Nutt, and an assistant, Joseph Wells, who became the proprietor in 1866 and the first eponymous bookseller. The bookshop's history is visible as soon as you step through the door: the mahogany counter, desks and shelving date back to 1889.

There are some high-profile ghosts inhabiting the place. This was Jane Austen's local bookshop – she lived two doors down, and is buried in the cathedral – and it's fun to imagine her walking around the place, picking out her favourite books. 'Did Jane Austen touch this? Let's pretend she touched this.' John Keats' 'Ode to Autumn' is set partly on

College Street, where P&G Wells is, so it's likely he used to visit, too. Charlotte Yonge and John Keble were nineteenth-century customers.

At the back of the bookshop there's something rather special: the bindery. It hasn't changed much over the years – in fact, a pair of huge eighteenth-century book-cutting shears still hang from the ceiling. Tim Wiltshire and his son Pete, who run the bindery, repair old books for the college, and other clients, as well as running workshops. 'The oldest book I've ever bound was an incunabulum from an apprentice of Caxton, a Wynkyn de Worde,' Tim told me. 'Sadly I've never repaired or bound a Caxton (the owner of the first moving printing press in Britain), though I have bound a continental book that pre-dates him, which would have been published in the 1400s.' Tim – who has a first edition of *Through the Looking-Glass* on a shelf next to his desk – has also handled books that once belonged to Elizabeth I, some signed 'Charles Dickens', as well as unbound manuscripts from a thousand years ago, and an old Greek *New Testament* that was a present to Thomas Cranmer from the Spanish ambassador. 'My favourites aren't necessarily the really old ones, though,' he says. 'The college has a great collection of Thackeray. Dickens and Thackeray were great mates, and Dickens would often send him copies of books, scribbling in the front, "This is a good one; I think you'll enjoy this," which is always fun to see. I've re-bound a few of those.'

P&G Wells is a rather special place, a fascinating mix of the old and the new. Throughout history it's been involved in the local community, printing and delivering newspapers and opening libraries. These days it's very involved with local schools, and still rebinding books for Winchester College, as well as providing its textbooks, as it has been since the 1700s. 'We've also been in close contact with the Austen Society,' says the Events Manager, Ben Tanter. 'You wouldn't think that after 250 years new people would still be discovering us, but they are, and it's great.'

❖

BOOKISH FACT

The Bosham Book Box in Sussex
is an old telephone box that's been
turned into a book swap.
It has had tiny bookshelves installed,
and is full of books. Locals can take
any book they want, so long as they
replace it with one of their own.
It is the UK's smallest lending library.

• A CHAT WITH NATHAN FILER •

Nathan Filer is a writer and lecturer in Creative Writing at Bath Spa University. His novel *The Shock of the Fall* won the 2013 Costa Book of the Year Award and has been sold in over twenty countries.

" As a child I refused to read anything. My parents were both avid readers, and my mum in particular was keen to see me bitten by the bug. The more she tried the harder I'd resist – I must hold a world record for the slowest, most laboured reading of *Flat Stanley*. I had a determined lack of interest. I don't suppose that's so unusual, especially for boys. We can put too much pressure on children to read. I believe there are more important things in life.

What I did enjoy was writing stories of my own. I remember when I was nine I set about trying to write a horror novel. Not a short story, but a whole novel, or, more to the point – a *book*. I think this makes sense, in a Freudian sort of way: I would see my parents reading; our house was full of books; books as objects fascinated me. My journey into reading came later. When I was a teenager a friend lent me *The Cement Garden* by Ian McEwan, and the penny finally dropped. *So* this *is what a novel can be…* I was astounded by it – still am, really. McEwan remains my favourite author.

Today my shelves are full, complete with a signed first edition of *The Cement Garden*. Five shelves below are all the books that my wife and I have been collecting for our baby daughter. Lots of C. S. Lewis, Beatrix Potter, A. A. Milne. She's still too young to read, but seems to enjoy them very much as objects. I must buy her *Flat Stanley*.

When I was six years old I wrote a story involving a horse-drawn canal boat. I'm a little vague on the plot now, but I can still picture very clearly the paper I wrote it on – the continuous, perforated

kind you used to find in dot-matrix printers. I remember this because I needed two whole sheets to fit my story on – without any
pictures – and this was a point of considerable pride. So I've been
writing all my life, but my career in writing started in my early
twenties on the performance poetry circuit. I wrote stand-up
shows, short films and bits and pieces for radio before returning
to my childhood dream to write a book. I read differently now. I
read as a writer. If I'm impressed by a paragraph or a sentence I
find myself re-reading it over and over, trying to unlock its secret.

Writing my novel was the biggest journey, emotionally and
cognitively, I have ever taken, and now it's a great pleasure to
walk into a bookshop and see it. Not in isolation, but beside so
many other works, each with the potential to amaze and con-
found, to transform or frustrate or bore. Each containing whole
lives. I've also come to learn something obvious: selling books is
a business. There are profit margins and marketing strategies and
a whole load of other stuff that we writers catch glimpses of from
the peripheries. Profit margins and marketing aside, it feels wonderful to be a part of that.

Book signings still befuddle me. I'm yet to perfect my 'author
signature'. I'm good right up to the last three letters, when a panic
grips me and anything can happen. At least they're unique. But,
technical difficulties aside, I do enjoy attending events,
and especially the Q&A sessions. It's great when someone makes
an observation about my novel that I had never considered
myself. I think there are as many versions of a story as there
are people who read it. My favourite signing was the first one
I ever did, at Topping & Company, a beautiful bookshop in
Bath which kindly offered to host my launch. It was special
because the shop was full to the rafters with family and
friends. After my reading, the queue formed. Never have
I signed so many books without asking a single name. 99

✶ ✶ ✶ SOME WONDERFUL THINGS ✶ ✶ ✶

◆ Ebb & Flo bookshop in Chorley has just opened and is determined to show the town why bookshops are important. Between them Diane and Martin, who run it, have previously worked in a library, schools, colleges, shops, a pie maker's and a fizzy pop factory. They say that opening a bookshop seemed the logical next step.

◆ Simply Books in Cheshire opened in 2002 and has won so many awards that a wall of the shop is dedicated to them. For the launch of *Harry Potter and the Deathly Hallows* owners Sue and Andrew hired a stately home and a group of actors, who came kitted out in wizard robes. Four hundred customers came along to enjoy the party.

◆ Classic Chaps in Iden, near Rye, sells bow ties, tweed jackets, top hats, cravats – and poetry books. Its proprietors are looking to breed a new line of dandies. I approve of this idea very much.

◆ Bookbarn International, near Bristol, is England's largest used book warehouse. The books are piled all the way up to the ceiling!

◆ The Big Comfy Bookshop, owned by Michael McEntee, is bucking the trend magnificently by transitioning from being an online-only bookshop to a bricks-and-mortar one. When Fargo Village opens in autumn 2014 near Coventry it will be a purpose-built cultural hub, with café, artist workshops, Michael's bookshop and more.

◆ Gothic Image in Glastonbury sells and publishes books on the power of the mind and the universe. They say that the ancient sacred sites near them have stories and mysteries to reveal, and now they want to share them.

◆ Boulevard Bookshop in Hastings is also a Thai restaurant. It doesn't have a separate dining area: the tables are all squeezed in between the bookshelves. So you can eat Tom Yam Kung and examine the books at the same time.

◆ Alice Harandon works at St Ives Booksellers in Cornwall, which is fitted with solid oak shelves and Cornish slate floors. One of the most bizarre moments she's had was when a squirrel ran in and started knocking books off the shelves. She and her customers spent a long time trying to chase it back out onto the street.

When I worked in a second-hand bookshop – so easily pictured, if you don't work in one, as a kind of paradise where charming old gentlemen browse eternally among calf-bound folios – the thing that chiefly struck me was the rarity of really bookish people...

Our shop stood exactly on the frontier between Hampstead and Camden Town, and we were frequented by all types from baronets to bus-conductors... Many of the people who came to us were of the kind who would be a nuisance anywhere but have special opportunities in a bookshop... There are two well-known types of pest by whom every second-hand bookshop is haunted. One is the decayed person smelling of old bread crusts who comes every day, sometimes several times a day, and tries to sell you worthless books. The other is the person who orders large quantities of books for which he has not the smallest intention of paying...

As soon as I went to work in the bookshop, I stopped buying books. Seen in the mass, five or ten thousand at a time, books were boring and even slightly sickening... The sweet smell of decaying paper appeals to me no longer. It is too closely associated in my mind with paranoiac customers and dead bluebottles.

from 'Bookshop Memories', *The Complete Works of George Orwell,* published by Harvill Secker.

◆

London

George Orwell's bookshop is no longer around, but I do recommend you find yourself a copy of the London Bookshop Map, a fantastic fold-out map pinpointing over 100 independent bookshops in the capital, created by Louise O'Hare. You can find a version of the London Bookshop Map online at thelondonbookshopmap.org, and physical copies are available to pick up for free in all of the bookshops on the map itself. Each new edition also links in with the text-based art of contemporary artists, the most recent of which, by Dora Garcia, is called 'Twenty-three million, five hundred and eighty-six thousand, four hundred and ninety stories', employing pieces of flash fiction created by users of the London Bookshop Map app.

◆

London Bookshop Facts

◆ The oldest bookshop in London still trading is Hatchards in Piccadilly, founded in 1797 by John Hatchard after he had acquired many books from the famous eighteenth-century bookseller Simon Vandenbergh.

◆ When Brunel's Thames Tunnel opened in 1843, Vandenbergh's grandson, John Vandenbergh Quick, also a bookseller, took on Stall 47 – a shop inside the tunnel itself. The first in the world to be constructed under a river, the Thames Tunnel was hailed as the eighth wonder of the world and people flocked to see it – 50,000 on the first day alone. Later in the century it was bought by the East London Railway Company and became part of the Underground network, but originally it was filled with stalls, along with performing horses and, strangely, a ballroom. A visitor coming out at the other end having bought many things whilst down there was considered a very brave person, as it meant they'd spent a lot of time down there. Naturally, the merchants who'd set up stalls along the

THE FANCY FAIR IN THE THAMES TUNNEL.

Tunnel thrived on all this, calling those who refused to buy things cowards as a way to get them to spend more money. John Vandenbergh Quick set up a printing press as well as a bookstall inside the Tunnel, printing souvenir broadsheets to commemorate the opening, and others to celebrate the queen's visit. 'Printed by Authority, 76 feet below high-water mark', they proclaimed in big letters: the world's first underwater printing press! Vandenbergh Quick is also often credited with the invention of the pop-up book, making elaborate peep-show books offering 3D optical illusions of the Thames Tunnel. He's reported to have lost his fortune trying to make world literature available to the poor in one-penny instalments. On a side note: when pickpocketing and debauchery meant trade in the Thames Tunnel became almost impossible, the tunnel was turned into the world's first underwater fairground instead. The Thames Tunnel Fancy Fair was opened in 1852 with fire-swallowers, tightrope artists, performing horses, Indian dancers, Chinese singers, Ethiopian serenaders... There were even steam-powered organs that filled the underground space with music and,

The Bookshop, Wigtown, UK.

Leakey's Bookshop, Inverness, UK.

Barter Books, Alnwick, UK.

The book bindery sewing room at George Bayntun in Bath, UK, 1940s.

The Book Barge, Lichfield, UK.

Sarah Henshaw and The Book Barge, Lichfield, UK.

© Tom Medwell

The Bookshop Band at Mr. B's Emporium of Reading Delights, Bath, UK.

George and Sylvia Whitman outside Shakespeare and Company, Paris.

Livraria Lello & Irmão, Porto, Portugal.

Cook & Book, Brussels, Belgium.

Urueña Book Town, Spain.

Tell a Story, Portugal.

Waanders in de Broeren, Zwolle, The Netherlands.

Selexyz Dominicanen, Maastricht, The Netherlands.

Libreria Palazzo Roberti, Italy.

Libreria Acqua Alta, Venice, Italy.

© Spiros Ionas

to the wonder of the visitors, there was also electricity. I think it's safe to say that the whole thing was slightly bizarre, but then the Victorians loved their circuses.

- Around the time of the Thames Tunnel Fancy Fair, booksellers in the 1800s were apparently not too fond of women, and unafraid to say so. *The Book-Hunter in London* by W. Roberts, published in 1895, has this to say about female book-collectors:

  'Bookstall keepers have a deep contempt for women who patronise them by turning over their books without purchasing. It would not be possible to repeat all the hard things they say about the sex. In the words of one: "They hang around and read the books, and though I have a man to watch them, while he is driving one away, another is reading a chapter"… The conclusion still forces itself upon one that the femme bibliophile is an all but unknown quantity. The New Woman may well develop into a genuine book-lover; it is certain the old one will not. The Chinese article of belief that women have no souls has, after all, something in its favour.'

- The Wapping Project, which ran until 2013, used an old power station in east London as an art space, and opened a bookshop in a greenhouse in the back garden.

- Camden Lock Books is a bookshop located in a subway underneath the Old Street roundabout.

- Along the South Bank, outside the BFI under Waterloo Bridge, you can still find the South Bank Book Market.

- London's oldest radical bookshop, Housmans, refused to close despite being offered huge amounts of money by developers.

- Book and Kitchen near Notting Hill is run by Muna Khogali; cakes are sold downstairs, and the bookshop sections are marked out using Scrabble letters.

- Skoob, at the Brunswick near Russell Square, is an underground bookshop holding 55,000 books. Its warehouse is in the basement; another, in Oxfordshire, contains a further one million titles.

- The Review Bookshop in Peckham is run by Evie Wyld, author of *All the Birds, Singing*. 'I get asked quite a lot how running a bookshop changes the way I write,' she says, 'and I don't really think it does. However, I do think that writing books has changed the way I sell them. I'm now more conscious of everything that goes into them: their text, covers, tag lines... I feel aware of all the people that one book represents.'

- In 2010, the Foldaway Bookshop sprang up in the centre of town, designed by Campaign. Open for only thirteen days, to coincide with the London Festival of Architecture, the whole shop was made out of cardboard, and was recycled when it closed. It stocked books on architecture, and the shelves were designed to look like the pages of an open book.

- Watermark Books, which opened a couple of years ago inside Kings Cross Station, is one of my favourite new bookshops in London. There isn't another bookshop in the world that, asked, 'Where can I find you?' can honestly answer: 'Right beside Platform 9¾.' So it is: there's a big sign and half a trolley embedded in the wall, with a constant queue of people waiting to take their photograph beside it.

- Charing Cross Road is the bookshop centre of London. Home of the book *84, Charing Cross Road*, it's especially famous for its second-hand and specialist bookshops, and is also where you can find Foyles. Sadly, rent increases have seen some bookshops close in recent years, but many remain, such as Claire de Rouen, a fashion, art and photography bookshop now run by Lucy Moore. When it hit financial difficulties a few years ago, the model and actress Lily Cole stepped in to help out, and is now part-owner.

- Cecil Court, a short street of bookshops branching off Charing Cross Road, has one of my favourite bookshops: Marchpane. As *Through the Looking-Glass* is my favourite book, it's a very dangerous place for me to go: they have hundreds of editions in many different languages. I'm not sure why I'm aching to own a copy of *Alice* in Arabic, considering I wouldn't be able to read it, but it does look very beautiful...

- Watkins on Cecil Court, which opened in 1893, is London's oldest occult bookshop, and Treadwells in Bloomsbury also specialise in the esoteric. The staff there includes a hedge witch and a shamanic practitioner, and the shelves are full of delightfully bizarre works on cryptozoology (the study of animals that haven't been proven to exist), as well as books about Aleister Crowley, Quimbanda, folklore, marsh wizards, and everything else to do with witchcraft you could possibly imagine. They also sell cauldrons, along with potion ingredients, and a large selection of wands. If the mood takes you, you can even buy snakeskin parchment.

❖

BOOKISH FACT

From 1913–1926 there was a bookshop
in central London called the Poetry
Bookshop. It had bookshop cats and dogs,
and not only sold poetry but published it,
too, including work by Ezra Pound.
Some poets, like Wilfred Owen and
Robert Frost, even lived in it for a while.
During the First World War its owner
Harold Monro had to serve in the armed
forces, so the bookshop was run by
his assistant, whom he later married.

◆

Foyles

I'm yet to meet someone who does not love Foyles. It has a fantastic history; they clearly love what they are doing, and the development of their new flagship store on Charing Cross Road has seen it labelled 'The Future Bookshop.'

Let's go back to the beginning. Foyles was set up in 1903 by two brothers, William and Gilbert, who had failed their Civil Service examinations. On a whim, they put an advert in the newspaper to sell off their textbooks, but even after they'd sold them they continued to receive enquiries, realised there was business to be had, and decided to buy more stock and keep going. Initially they sold books out of their mother's kitchen, before moving to Cecil Court a year later, and by 1906 they were on Charing Cross Road. Thirty years after that, they had a stock of five million books on thirty miles of shelving.

Over the years Foyles have branched out into many different areas. They've had a travel bureau and a handicraft shop. In the thirties they started 'Foyles Libraries', which consisted of over 3,000 two-penny libraries – a cheap alternative to other subscription libraries – not just in Britain but as far away as Palestine and Australia. There were even a few on ocean liners. By the 1950s, Foyles was a book publisher, while the Foyles Entertainment Department hired out entertainment for parties.

The majority owner is now Christopher Foyle, who took over the shop from his legendary and eccentric aunt, Christina Foyle. He has some amazing stories to tell. Foyles once sued the Pope for non-payment of bills, for instance, and in the 1930s a lady used to run the Occult section of the bookshop with her pet parrot perched on her shoulder. No-one minded too much until the parrot attacked one of the customers.

'I grew up steeped in Foyles,' Christopher told me. 'My aunt Christina and my grandfather were aware that lots of interesting, famous people would come into the shop. So Christina thought that it would be nice to organise luncheons for authors, especially for book launches, which we could ticket and charge people to come along to. The first one was on 30 October 1930: Christina invited Conan Doyle, H. G. Wells and George Bernard Shaw, but they all turned her down. George Bernard Shaw said that she'd have to hire the Royal Albert Hall if she wanted to invite all his admirers, and H. G. Wells said he'd read letters from his fans and had no desire to meet any of them in person, thank you very much. The luncheons became such a success over the years that those three did eventually eat their words and accept invitations to come along.

'I can remember the very first lunch I ever went to, as it was action-packed. It was for the great editor of the *Daily Mirror* at the time, Hugh Cudlipp, and the man in the chair was Randolph Churchill, Winston Churchill's son. It's the chairman's job to get up and make a speech about the author the lunch is for, praising them and their work. But Randolph Churchill had a bit too much to drink, and when he got up to make the speech, instead of praising Hugh Cudlipp, he went on a drunken rampage and called him all sorts of names, one of which was "The Pornographer Royal"! So when Hugh Cudlipp got up to make his speech, he ripped up his notes and instead launched into a violent attack on Randolph Churchill, saying that if he wasn't the son of a famous man then he wouldn't be there chairing the event at all. It was all frightfully dramatic and, I thought, highly amusing. I couldn't really understand everything that was going on, of course, as I think I was about ten at the time, but I remember asking my aunt afterwards what a pornographer was, and she said, straight-faced, "It's somebody who plays a pornograph."'

Christopher started working in Foyles in December 1961, and worked until August the following year. His interest was archaeology and anthropology, which Foyles didn't have sections for, so he created those departments himself. After that, he went to Europe to learn about the book trade there. He worked in a German publishing house, and then a bookshop in Finland, where he lived with a lighthouse keeper. Then he headed to Paris, where he worked in Galignani in rue de Rivoli (the first English bookshop opened on the continent), run and owned by a direct descendant of the booksellers who had started trading in Italy in 1520. Later, when working for an educational French publisher, Christopher went to Normandy to see how the paper was made. 'I was told the most horrific story,' says Christopher:

'Paper starts out being liquid, in a massive vat, with blades going round and round. It comes out, dries and goes through rollers to become paper sheets. One day they couldn't find one of the men working in the mill, and it turned out that he'd fallen into the vat, and been chopped up and turned into paper. They had to burn the roll of paper they thought was most likely to contain him. A horrible thought, really, and I'll admit it took a little romance out of book-making for a while.'

After travelling around Russia, Christopher decided to head back to the UK and leave the book business to set up his own aviation company, which became very successful. Then in 1999, six days before she died, Christina Foyle asked him to come back to Foyles, to become the sole director. Under her ownership, there had been many strikes by the staff, and by the 1980s customers were becoming annoyed with some of the more eccentric aspects of the business. Christina hated change, explained Christopher: the stock was arranged according to publisher, instead of in alphabetical order; for a long time, Christina had refused to install a telephone; and, just to pay for a book, customers had to queue at three separate counters to complete their transactions. 'The shop was in desperate need of shaking up,' he admits. 'The figures weren't looking good, and staff morale was down. Ever since then we've been turning it around.'

On Christopher's return, Foyles set about growing its business again. When Europe's leading feminist bookshop, Silver Moon, had to close due to a rent increase, Foyles bought the company to run it as a shop within their own premises. When Ray's Jazz, a much-loved music shop, faced the same fate, Foyles bought them too and invited them to set up inside the store and theme their cafe. These days it even offers literary tours of London, run by authors. At the beginning of 2014, Foyles opened a new branch in Waterloo station, and later that year they completed their new flagship store, two doors down from their previous home on Charing Cross Road in the building vacated by St Martin's art college.

What was going to be in it? How exactly was it going to be The Bookshop of the Future? There were rumours flying around the publishing trade of spaceship-like reading pods, flying books and secret author rooms... Foyles asked others in the industry, as well as their own staff and customers, what they wanted from a new bookshop. As a result, the new building has been designed with an atrium, from which customers can see several floors of books stretching away above them. There's a café, a gallery, and an event space, and each section of the shop has a slightly different design so that readers can move between reading environments to find the one that suits them best. The grand opening of the bookshop was celebrated with a three-week festival, with authors ceremonially opening up different sections of the store.

Its aim is to be *the* meeting place in central London, and to cater both for those who want to talk to booksellers and get advice, and those who want to wander around on their own. For the latter, they're producing an app that will allow customers to use their phones as a tracking device to find the book they're after once they're in store. Using this technology in turn to input booksellers' knowledge and create more detailed algorithms for book recommendations would offer something online sites are unable to do. They say this is not to replace the role of booksellers but to work alongside them. 'The world of bookselling should be a place of constant correction,' says Sion Hamilton, Foyles' Retail Operations Director. 'We have to keep talking to people, and adjusting what we do based on the ever-changing industry. We have to constantly evolve. I find it very exciting. It's true when people quote William Gibson: "The future is already here – it's just not evenly distributed yet."'

◆

Daunt Books

James Daunt, listed by the *Guardian* as one of the top five most influential people in the British book industry, admits he moved from banking to bookselling over twenty years ago for love. Not just for the love of books, but because his then girlfriend wasn't happy with the long hours he was working as a banker. So, after quitting his job and considering his main interests in life (reading and travelling), he founded Daunt Books and opened their first branch in 1990. Housed in a former Edwardian bookshop in Marylebone, with stained glass windows, oak balconies and William Morris prints, Daunt Books has become the leading travel and literary bookshop in London, now with six branches across the city. (My favourite part of the bookshop in the Marylebone branch is downstairs, where they've arranged translated novels and poetry collections by country of origin. You can regularly find me rummaging through the Japan section.)

Approaching bookselling as someone who worked in finance, James admits that he looked at other bookshops and saw a lot of people 'doing it badly,' as well as noting that bookselling was, and still is, a difficult industry to succeed in.

'I took the lease on Daunt Books in the financial bubble of the late eighties,' he explains. 'Just before the recession of the early nineties, so it was certainly a test. I had to work out how to do things differently; without wanting to sound too obnoxious, I wanted to make a living from bookselling. The way to do that, as far as I was concerned, was to really invest in the people who worked in my bookshop. The key to good staff is to keep them long term; to build their careers; to teach them the trade. I think that the intelligent, pro-active people who make good booksellers also make good bookshops. The common practice in chain bookselling at the time (for instance with Ottaker's and Waterstones) was to hire people for short periods of time and pay them as little as possible. That wasn't something that I wanted to do.'

In May 2011, James Daunt also became the managing director of Waterstones, answering a plea from them to try and save the company in an ever-changing, and Amazon-dominated, market. He accepted the challenge, and has since implemented a massive restructuring of the Waterstones management system, in a bid to make each bookshop run more effectively, with tighter teams and stronger leadership. Waterstones have also rolled out their own café, Café W, and plan to open several new branches across the UK. Somewhat controversially, James Daunt also signed a deal with Amazon, to sell their Kindle in Waterstones stores.

'It was a difficult move,' James admits: 'To invite our competitor to sell their products in our space, but my predecessor hadn't thought to invest in creating Waterstones e-readers, or to negotiate with other e-reader companies with a view to sell their products. W.H. Smith had the Kobo, Blackwell's had the Nook; it was clear that we had to make a move quickly, or we would lose our chance to take part in the rapidly expanding e-book market. Agreeing to sell Kindle was making the best of a bad situation, and my feeling is that we are selling Kindles to people who would be buying them anyway. It's clearly not an ideal situation to be in, but we had to do it.

'E-books don't mean the end of physical bookshops. There is still a place for bookshops, or rather a retail space that sells books and is also an engaging, compelling environment. I cannot believe that e-books sales are going to expand in a way that will crush the market. At the moment publishers talk about a 70%-30% split (the 30% being digital), some a little higher but not by much. We can definitely see figures in the States leveling out, with sales of e-books slowing down, and print sales rising. If you own something digital, you don't own a physical thing. I can see e-books replacing the paperback copies one might give away after a single read, but I still think that people like to *own* books – physical books and beautiful objects – and, because of that, good bookshops will stay.

'As for children, they are still reading. I have children of my own, and they love books. If you fall in love with reading young, it's something that will stay with you throughout your whole life – you might not find yourself reading all of the time, but you will always go through periods of wanting to be around books, and the worlds that they offer. The world of books and bookshops is a very stimulating one, full of interesting and wonderful people, be it writers, booksellers, agents, publishers or customers. Because of this, good bookshops often become hubs of local communities, and I sincerely hope that they continue to do so.'

• A CHAT WITH JACQUELINE WILSON •

Jacqueline Wilson is one of the best-selling children's writers in the UK, where her books have sold over 35 million copies. She has won the Children's Book Award, the Smarties Prize and the Guardian Children's Fiction Award. Jacqueline was Children's Laureate from 2005–2007 and became a Dame in 2008.

" I loved books long before I could read. I only had a handful of picture books, but I'd turn the pages and mutter my own stories to go along with the illustrations. I learned to read fluently by the time I was six, and then I frequently read a book a day. I practically lived in the local library, and spent my pocket money on Puffin paperbacks.

The only bookshop we had in Kingston long ago when I was a little girl was a W.H. Smith. It only had a few shelves of children's books in those days – but I still begged to go and look at them every time I went shopping with my mum. Then one year she took me up to London and we went to Foyles – a bookshop beyond my wildest dreams. It had a very big second-hand section at that time, so I had more chance of being bought a present! By the time I was nine or ten, second-hand bookshops had become my passion. My father took me to Guildford every summer for a long walk in the country – but first we stopped off at an amazing old bookshop at the top of the High Street, with seemingly hundreds of rooms crammed with dusty old books. There was a special room devoted to children's books, and if I'd been very good I was allowed to choose one. It's sadly closed down now, along with many other fantastic second-hand bookshops. Browsing on the internet isn't the same at all! I used to go to a magical book warehouse in Surbiton as a young married woman, spending half my housekeeping money on first editions and nineteenth-century children's books.

I've always enjoyed doing events in specialist children's bookshops, like the Muswell Hill Children's Bookshop, and the late, lamented Lion and Unicorn in Richmond. My favourite local bookshop is also in Richmond, the Open Book. Helena manages to cram her small premises with an astonishing amount of beautiful books and I never go out of there empty handed. Going further afield, I love visiting the Much Ado bookshop in Alfriston, run by Cate and Nash – especially near Christmas when Cate gift-wraps every purchase and makes special Christmas stockings and all kinds of festive novelties (see page 57). I love independent bookshops, but I've also been a fan of Waterstones ever since they first opened – I was especially fond of the London branch that had two resident cats, Boswell and Johnson. Whenever I do an event in a Waterstones now I know it will be brilliantly organised and a big success.

I think bookshops and libraries are vital. It seems so sad that so many libraries have been closed down and so many bookshops have disappeared. If children can't see books on shelves and learn to enjoy browsing before they select a book then they'll never become keen readers.

Imagining my own bookshop is a favourite fantasy. I'd have a second-hand children's bookshop and I'd do my best to make it as child-friendly as possible. I'd shelve the books by subject as well as alphabetically – so I'd bunch all books about rabbits together (Peter Rabbit, *Little Grey Rabbit*, Brer Rabbit, *Watership Down*, etc.) and put a real rabbit in a state-of-the-art hutch by this section. Then I'd bunch together books about dolls and dolls' houses with a display of actual dolls; I'd prop a carpet bag and a parrot-headed umbrella by all the Mary Poppins stories; I'd put a drawing pad and pencils by the Wimpy Kid books, so that children could do their own stickman illustrations... I could go on! ''

PERSEPHONE BOOKS

Persephone Books is a publishing house that reprints neglected fiction and non-fiction for women, about women, and mainly by women. Its books are renowned for their beautiful design (sleek grey covers and high-quality paper), and the small bookshop Persephone runs in the heart of Bloomsbury, that sits in the same room as its publishing office, is just as beautiful as the books themselves. 'I think publishers having a bookshop, taking things back to their roots, is a great idea,' says Persephone's owner Nicola Beauman. 'I don't understand why more publishers don't do it. We started the bookshop in 2001, and I really like the hands-on aspect of it. Not to mention that we know the ins and outs of every single book we stock, simply because we've produced them. That makes us quite passionate, and unique.'

'One of my favourite things,' adds Alice who works at Persephone, 'is when customers leave messages for us to copy out on to gift cards to send with the books. It's a little glimpse into people's relationships not only with the books, but with each other, and that's rather lovely.'

" Ripping Yarns is one of the last remaining treasure troves of second-hand bookshops. I never fail to find something amazing, whether it be a forgotten book from my childhood, memorabilia or poetry I could not find anywhere else. It is always an adventure to step inside and come home with books I love. "

Deborah Levy, author of the Man Booker-shortlisted novel *Swimming Home*

♦

Ripping Yarns

I'm a little biased when it comes to Ripping Yarns, because I worked there. I stumbled across the shop when I moved down to London after graduating. I couldn't help but be lured in by the massive cut-out illustration of Alice in the window.

Previously located in north London opposite Highgate tube station, Ripping Yarns now runs from the bookshop owner's house and is a second-hand and antiquarian bookshop that specialises in children's books, but it stocks pretty much anything and everything.

It's been a bookshop since the 1930s, and Celia Hewitt has been running it since the 1980s. 'I was an actress – well, I still am an actress,' Celia explains, 'and I used to do a lot of touring. I spent a lot of my time in second-hand bookshops all over the place. I accumulated all different kinds of Victorian books, as well as schoolgirls' books such as Angela Brazil, and childhood favourites like *Biggles* and *Jennings*. And then when I was out of work, someone advertised for help in an antique shop on Archway Road. It was next door to a run-down bookshop from the 1930s that had recently closed down.

'While working at the antique shop, I found that people would come with suitcases full of books, looking for the bookshop next door in the hope of selling them. Partly out of curiosity, I eventually started buying them, and in the end I had so many that I decided to take on the lease of the derelict bookshop. We re-designed it, painted it, and in the window we had a model of *Just William*, because I had a lot of William books. We haven't got him any more because he got very old and dirty. I put him in the outside rubbish bin and it scared the dustbin men out of their wits!

'I had no idea how to run a business, but my husband and I both loved books. He was a writer and a poet [Adrian Mitchell], and whenever he had a new book out, usually near Christmas, he'd come in to the shop to do a reading. When I bought books for the shop, he would to go through them first and say, "No, I need that one; I need it for research." I did say to him that he wasn't going to live long enough to write all the plays that he wanted, and in fact he didn't, but he loved collecting the books all the same.

'At the time I got the bookshop we were living in Hampstead, and these two jolly Australian girls turned up on our doorstep looking for work. So they helped us out minding the children and made cakes for the bookshop, and we had a big press launch for its reopening. Michael Palin and Terry Jones came and opened the bookshop for me because Ripping Yarns, of course, was the name of their television series. They both read aloud from *Biggles* and *Just William* books, and I think I made a lot of money that night – and not much since!

'We do sometimes get odd customers, but then most bookshops do. We've even had several stalkers in the past. One was obsessed with gardening, and he'd come in and speak to Zoë, a very beautiful girl who used to work here, who had never really been to the countryside and knew nothing about gardening. Anyway, he used to come in here repeatedly and ask her lots of questions about tractors, even though he knew she didn't know the answers!

'However, we all love books and that's the main thing, and we have quite a jolly time. A lot of actresses have worked for me, as well as musicians, writers and artists – people in the arts, really. We sell books to all kinds of people: once we even did a bulk sale to help stock a children's library in Japan!'

One day at the bookshop I got a call from a lady who had spied a collection of nature tales on our online inventory. She used to have the book when she was younger, she said, but her mother had sold her copy at a jumble sale forty years ago without her permission, and recently she'd been hoping to track down a copy to read to her grandchildren. She'd never forgotten the beautiful colour plates, protected with tissue paper, that she'd lift gently to peer underneath when no-one else was looking, as though the book was hiding secrets. She was thrilled to find we had a copy. I packaged the book up and posted it to her.

The next day she called me back. I quickly realised she was in tears, and I worried that the book might have got damaged in the mail. No-one wants a squashed book. But it turned out that the book I had posted to her was *her* book: the actual copy, with the inscription in the front from her great aunt, and one of the corners bumped from where she'd dropped it down the stairs when she was seven. Forty years ago, some 200 miles away, her mother had sold the book, and somehow we'd come across it and somehow she'd come across us, and there she was, reunited with her very own book. It's moments like this that make bookselling one of the best jobs in the world.

But here, none too soon, are the second-hand bookshops...
Books are everywhere; and always the same sense of adventure
fills us. Second-hand books are wild books, homeless books;
they have come together in vast flocks of variegated feather,
and have a charm which the domesticated volumes of the
library lack. Besides, in this random miscellaneous company
we may rub against some complete stranger who will, with
luck, turn into the best friend we have in the world. There is
always a hope, as we reach down some grayish-white book
from an upper shelf, directed by its air of shabbiness and
desertion, of meeting here with a man who set out on
horseback over a hundred years ago to explore the woollen
market in the Midlands and Wales; an unknown traveller,
who stayed at inns, drank his pint, noted pretty girls and
serious customs, wrote it all down stiffly, laboriously for
sheer love of it...

The number of books in the world is infinite, and one is
forced to glimpse and nod and move on after a moment of
talk, a flash of understanding, as, in the street outside, one
catches a word in passing and from a chance phrase
fabricates a lifetime.

Virginia Woolf, from 'Street-haunting: A London Adventure'

• A CHAT WITH SCOTT PACK •

Scott Pack is a publisher at the Friday Project at HarperCollins. He used to be the Head Buyer for Waterstones, and the *Guardian* once declared him the most powerful man in the book trade. He's also the author of several books, including *21st-Century Dodos*, under the pseudonym Steve Stack.

" There's a bookshop in Essex called Leigh Gallery Books, and when I first left home and had a flat around there I loved this bookshop because it did all the things I think good second-hand bookshops should do: they had a bookcase of orange Penguins; they put all of their Everyman hardbacks on the same shelf; and they sold jazz vinyl. I bought a book there that changed my life: *A Wild Sheep Chase* by Haruki Murakami. It was a hardback with a sheep on the front, peering out from behind a tree, wearing a Columbo coat: I just had to buy it. After reading just ten or twenty pages I thought: 'This is the author I've been looking for forever.' I also bought four volumes of a very old dictionary that was completely falling apart. I've used the pages as Christmas wrapping paper for years.

There's also a bookshop on the Isle of Wight I love called Ryde Bookshop. There are three floors of books, with each floor having three or four rooms stocking different genres. There's a children's room, a music room, a history room, and when I go to the Isle of Wight on holiday with my family, we take a whole afternoon to go to the bookshop and rummage around.

I think people in general have special connections with second-hand bookshops because we judge them differently. We go into a new bookshop and rule out 90% of the stock before we've even looked around; when we go into a second-hand bookshop, we think *anything* in there could be amazing. We know that things will be a little bit messy; we know there might be books piled up on the floor; but we also know it's going to be an adventure going through everything, looking at old inscriptions, and at hilariously out-of-date texts. We don't know what we're going to find, but we do know that the possibilities are endless. "

Wales

◆

Hay-on-Wye

When Richard Booth graduated from Oxford University, he decided to use money he had inherited to buy an old fire station in the small market town of Hay-on-Wye. The economy in Hay wasn't great, and he hoped that he could save it with the help of literature, so he turned the old fire station into a bookshop. Richard and his friends journeyed far and wide – all the way to America – to buy second-hand books and ship them back home to his shop. The idea of bookselling soon caught on, as others in the town started doing the same, and booksellers moved there from all across the UK. In the 1970s, Hay-on-Wye was established as 'The Town of Books', and has become the model for Book Towns all around the world. (See page 125 and 127) In 1977, Richard Booth initiated a publicity stunt by declaring Hay-on-Wye an independent kingdom, with himself as the King and his horse as Prime Minister. Extensive press coverage saw the issue of passports follow, and in 2000 Booth followed up by naming several people in Hay as lords of the kingdom.

When driving into Hay, you first come to the Children's Bookshop, which is a mile out of town and full to the brim with Enid Blytons and old school girls' annuals. Judith, who runs it, and her husband, who was a watchmaker, actually built the shop themselves. Further on, in the centre of the town there's the Cinema Bookshop – a bookshop in a converted cinema; Ashbrook Garage, which sells books on cars; Fleur de Lys, which sells books on trains; Book Passage – a corridor of books; Mostly Maps (I think you can guess what they sell there) and the Broad Street Book Centre, which houses the stock of twenty different booksellers under one roof. Hay-on-Wye has twenty-five bookshops in total, with a few open by appointment only, and two bookbinders as well. Richard Booth's Bookshop now has a café and a cinema inside it, and he also owns a bookshop up the road called The King of Hay. At the crime bookshop, Murder and Mayhem, their own green Penguin Crime cover is posted in the window: *The Kindle Crack'd from Side to Side*. The interior is a little like a game of Cluedo, with fake weapons lying around on bookshelves and the white outline of a man drawn on the floor.

I'd expected the Poetry Bookshop – the only bookshop in the UK dedicated to poetry – to be small, considering its specialism, but it wasn't: an entire staircase of translated poetry leads down into a basement, as well as the packed shelves on the floor above. Chris, the owner, once had some-one call the shop to tell him they'd been writing poetry for quite a while, and felt they should be getting paid for it, so demanded Chris pay them an hourly rate to write. Baffled, Chris had to explain that that's not quite how the industry works. Though from strange things customers say, to odd things booksellers do: Chris has done something I fear I might do one day: accidentally lock a customer in the bookshop. However, it was only during lunch, not overnight and, besides, there are worse things in life than being locked inside a bookshop.

◆

Pendleburys, Porthyrhyd

Pendleburys bookshop is in the middle of a forest, on a converted hill farm. Its owner, John Pendlebury, has been selling books since he was fourteen, and ran a bookshop in London for thirty-two years. His Welsh bookshop, housed in a barn, sells second-hand and antiquarian books on pretty much all subjects, though it specialises in theology and hor-ticulture. John and his team also work the land, and are currently creating a three-acre garden to open to the public, where they plan to sell antiquarian gardening tools, too.

In the summer of 1997 Pendleburys had a problem: a book thief. They had no idea who was taking books from the shelves, but happily a friend who was holidaying in Spain helped them out. He sent John a copy of an ancient curse he'd found, believed to have originated in the Monastery of San Pedro in Barcelona, that was specifically intended for book thieves:

For him that stealeth a book from this library, let it change into a serpent in his hand and rend him. Let him be struck with palsy and all his members blasted. Let him languish in pain, crying aloud for mercy and let there be no surcease to his agony till he sink in Dissolution. Let Bookworms gnaw his entrails in token of the worm that dieth not, and when at last he goeth to his final punishment, let the flames of Hell consume him for ever and aye.

For amusement more than anything else, John decided to put the curse up on a placard in the bookshop …and it worked! Books stopped disappearing from the shelves. Volumes were even returned in the post with hastily handwritten notes of apology. Some of the books John received were never even his to begin with.

'It was rather funny,' he says. 'We wrote a short letter to the *Church Times* telling them about this phenomenon, and asked if any readers knew of a similar curse that might induce sales. We were much surprised when Thursday's copy of the *Church Times* arrived on our desk, delivered an hour early by the local newsagent, with our story on the front page. All very good we thought, and rather a laugh.

'The following morning the newsagent delivered both *The Times* and the *Telegraph* two hours early, as they both contained lead stories about our shop and the bookseller curse. When we tuned into Radio Four at 7 a.m. our names were mentioned in the press reviews, and this was quickly followed by calls from the BBC, ITV, and other independent stations. We decided not to open the shop that day due to the number of reporters at the front door. It was when faxes and telephone calls began to arrive from Spain, Ireland, the United States, Brazil and Mexico that we thought perhaps this story had gone a little too far – because we also had threatening messages from book thieves worried about their life expectancy!'

❖

BOOKISH FACT

Anthropodermic bibliopegy is the art of binding books in human skin. Father Henry Garnet, who was part of the 1605 Gunpowder Plot to blow up the Houses of Parliament, was sentenced to death by being drawn and quartered, after which the skin from his face was used to bind the book that listed the crimes against him. On more than one occasion in America, early in the nineteenth century, courts bound the transcript of a murder trial with the skin of the murderer after he had been executed. In 1877 the French astronomer Camille Flammarion had his book *Les Terres du Ciel* (*The Worlds of the Sky*), bound with the skin of a female admirer, which she had donated to him on her death.

Ireland

◆ The Winding Stair Bookshop & Café is one of the oldest surviving bookshops in Dublin. It's named after a Yeats poem and was saved from closure by Elaine Murphy in 2006, who now runs a restaurant on the floor above it. It overlooks the river Liffey and is a key meeting-place for writers and artists in the city.

◆ The Kenny family in Galway have been selling books since the 1940s. They also run an art gallery and Kenny's Bindery, which celebrated its fortieth anniversary in 2014. They use calf and goatskin and handmade marbled papers, and the books are finished by hand. The embossed leather is covered with a mixture of glycerine and egg white, a method used in bookbinding since the sixteenth century.

• A CHAT WITH JOHN CONNOLLY •

John Connolly was born in Dublin in 1968 and has at various points in his life worked as a journalist, a barman, a local government official, a waiter and a dogsbody at Harrods department store in London. He is the author of, amongst other books, the Charlie Parker mysteries, the Samuel Johnson novels, *The Book of Lost Things* and, with his partner Jennifer Ridyard, is co-author of *The Chronicles of the Invaders*.

" I think books captured me from the moment that my pre-primary school teacher, Mrs Foley, handed out our first readers. It was *Tom and Nora*, and *Spot the Dog*, and each of us was given one to take home. I can remember catching on quickly, just as I can recall the first book I ever read alone: it was a Secret Seven novel by Enid Blyton, and I can still see myself at the table in our living room, trying to work my way through the longer words phonetically, to the extent that for years after I thought the word 'cupboard' was pronounced 'cup-board'. My mother must have thought she was living with Little Lord Fauntleroy: 'Can I get something from the cup-board, momma?'

Shortly after I'd got the hang of reading, that same Mrs Foley would give me 5p for writing Tarzan stories, and 5p bought two bags of popcorn and two Fu Manchew chewing gums, which I'd share with my friend Brian Carroll on our way home from school at the end of the week. The Tarzan stories were only four or five pages long, but that's still a decent length for a six-year-old. Eventually I set out on my magnum opus, which was a long story featuring Casey Jones, the steam engine driver in the Old West, whose adventures I'd watch on TV on Saturday mornings. That one was huge: I think we're talking twenty or thirty pages, and I may have received as much as 50p for it. In the end, I owe everything to that schoolteacher.

My mother was the big reader in the house, and she made sure that I was sorted with a library ticket as soon as I began showing any interest in books. It strikes me now that I tend to buy all of my books new, whereas back then, because I had so little money, I relied almost entirely on the library and whatever I could trawl from sales and cheap bookstores. When I got my first proper job – with Dublin City Council, aged seventeen, I believe – I spent most of my first cheque on new books from the Penguin Bookshop in Dublin. I'd picked out the ones I wanted weeks beforehand, and I still think that going in on that Friday afternoon and spending that money was one of the happiest experiences of my life. I bought *The Great Shark Hunt* by Hunter S. Thompson; Mishima on Hagakure; *Doctor Zhivago* by Boris Pasternak; and a paperback library of Oxford reference books, including a decent dictionary and thesaurus. I'd never spent so much money on books before, because I never had it to spend.

A woman once came up to me at a crime convention in the US and enthused at some length about how much she loved my work. She then asked me to stay where I was so that she could go back to her room and pick up one of my books for me to sign. When she came back, she handed me a copy of *Black and Blue* by Ian Rankin.

I love the Rare Books Room at the Strand Bookstore in New York (see page 205), mainly because so much curious stuff passes through there, a lot of it signed, and they don't gouge on prices. I'm hugely fond of No Alibis, the mystery bookshop on Botanic Avenue in Belfast, where often the first thing you're offered when you step inside is a cup of tea and a biscuit. And if I had unlimited funds I'd haunt Mystery Pier in Los Angeles, which on a square-foot basis probably has more astonishing old books under its roof than anywhere else I've ever been. One of my loveliest recent discoveries is the Battery Park Book Exchange & Champagne Bar in Asheville, North Carolina, which is a huge new and used bookstore with an amazing wine bar inside. I mean, how much better can life get than a bookstore with a bar attached to it? I liked it so much I put it in *The Wolf in Winter*.

In the future, I think bookshops will essentially be independents, or part of a small chain. Their USP will be their specialist knowledge, and the shelves will be dotted with personal recommendations from booksellers. Most will have a coffee shop, and offer downloads as well as physical books. Most of their stock will be signed, or come with extra material or additions that you can't get with a download. What's important is that they survive, along with libraries, as brick-and-mortar entities. It's crucial that they're part of the visible fabric of our lives, as much for this generation as future ones. We learn by what we see around us, and that's what arouses our curiosity. Otherwise books will just become part of the general noise of games, downloaded films, Twitter, Facebook (or whatever comes after them), and films on the internet of people falling over. All those things, because they essentially involve skimming and moving quickly along to the next shiny bauble, are the antithesis of reading, which requires immersion. It worries me that we assume the same piece of technology – a tablet, for now – can offer both skimming and immersive experiences, because eventually skimming will win out. **"**

• A CHAT WITH EMMA DONOGHUE •

Emma Donoghue, an Irish writer living in Canada, is best known for her international bestseller *Room*. Her latest novel, a murder story set in 1870s San Francisco, is *Frog Music* (2014). www.emmadonoghue.com

" I remember my annual trips to a bookshop after Christmas, with one or more book tokens in hand. A crisp book token seemed much more valuable than cash, because it was purely for my pleasure; nobody could expect me to save it like pocket money, or spend it on birthday presents for any of my family of eight. I would spend hours weighing up the agonising choice – the thickness of these paperbacks, the prices, what I knew of the authors – before staggering home with a sackful. Although I was always a keen library user, buying books was a different order of bliss, because I would get to live with these ones. **"**

❖

Bookish Fact

Back in the day, to try and prevent people stealing books, this aggressive inscription was often written inside:

Steal not this book, my worthy friend,
For fear the gallows will be your end;
Up the ladder, and down the rope,
There you'll hang until you choke;
Then I'll come along and say –
'Where's that book you stole away?'

France

◆

Paris

Ah, Paris. The city of love and food and books. Abundant with literary cafés and penniless poets. Home of Le Procope, the city's oldest restaurant still trading, founded in 1686, where Voltaire is supposed to have drunk forty cups of coffee a day.

Also home to Bar Hemingway, at the Ritz Paris Hotel. So called because, when the Nazis surrendered their control over the city on 25 August 1944, Ernest Hemingway was nearby, working as a war correspondent, and was desperate to 'officially' liberate somewhere. There are many different accounts of this – one being that he was late because he'd been too busy filling his car with champagne – but the one I like best has it that Hemingway arrived at the hotel, ran up on to the roof and fired a round of shots into the sky, before haring back down to the bar. Declaring the hotel liberated from the Nazis, he then ordered fifty martinis to be shared out amongst the guests. Apparently the martinis weren't that great: the barman couldn't be located, and they had to mix the drinks themselves.

All along the right bank of the river Seine, from Pont Marie to the Quai du Louvre, and on the left bank from the Quai de la Tournelle to Quai Voltaire, you can find the Bouquinistes. These are second-hand and antiquarian bookselling stalls which were set up by travelling pedlars in the sixteenth century. In the next century the pedlars were driven out of the city and made to re-apply for their stalls, to ensure they met censorship regulations. Strict rules of this sort didn't go away: in 1810 Napoleon made all booksellers apply for a licence to trade. They had to hand in four morality references, to be certified by their local mayor, to prove they weren't planning to sell rebellious publications.

These days France still has the equivalent of the UK's old Net Book Agreement, meaning that discounting new books is banned – bar a 5%

discount for students – and its current Culture Minister, Aurélie Filippetti, is determined to help bookshops thrive. On my most recent visit to Paris in 2013 there were at least twenty bookshops scattered around our hotel, and it was lucky for my bank balance that most of these only stocked books in French. A particularly lovely bookshop is Le Monte en l'Air, which serves as bookshop, café and gallery. The Abbey Bookstore, at the other end of the scale, is a second-hand English bookshop so full of books I wonder if it isn't breaking the laws of physics. To my amazement, I discovered that there are bookshelves *behind* its bookshelves: the bookcases on the wall slide sideways, like French windows, revealing layers of books beneath.

My favourite place of all, though, is Shakespeare and Company.

◆

Shakespeare and Company, Paris

> " I would be happy to get older and older coming to Shakespeare and Co. When my skin has the look of leaves that have lain too long in the sun. When I am less certain, upright, ready, then the books will still be here. I can lean on them. "
>
> Jeanette Winterson, *An English Room*

In 1917 an American woman called Sylvia Beach came to Paris to study French literature. She stumbled across La Maison des Amis des Livres, a bookshop run by Adrienne Monnier, a French poet and publisher who was one of the first women in France to open her own bookshop. As was common in those days, Adrienne also ran a subscription library out of her shop, which Sylvia joined. The two became great friends and were later in a relationship, living together for over thirty years.

Adrienne inspired Sylvia to open her own bookshop, which she called Shakespeare and Company. Initially it was tiny, but in May 1921 it moved to 12 rue de l'Odéon, opposite Adrienne's bookshop, where it flourished. Sylvia's main aim was to make her bookshop a space for writers to come and congregate, and come they did. Authors such as Ernest Hemingway, T. S. Eliot, Ezra Pound and F. Scott Fitzgerald were regulars, and James Joyce even used the bookshop as his office. Sylvia became Joyce's secretary, editor and publisher, printing *Ulysses* when English and American publishers had refused to on grounds of obscenity.

During the occupation of Paris in the early 1940s, a Nazi soldier came to Shakespeare and Company and tried to buy a copy of *Finnegan's Wake*. Sylvia refused to serve him. The officer said he would come back with his troops and burn the whole place down so, as soon as he left, Sylvia and her friends hastily removed all the books from the shop, and boarded it up. She never re-opened.

In 1951 another American moved to Paris to open an English bookshop. This was George Whitman, and his bookshop was called Le Mistral. He opened it on the Left Bank, right next to Notre Dame, in a building that was once part of a sixteenth-century monastery. Like Sylvia's bookshop before it, Le Mistral became a hub for writers – in fact George often called it a social utopia masquerading as a bookshop. In 1964, after Sylvia Beach's death, George changed the name of Le Mistral to Shakespeare and Company in her honour.

From the 1970s onwards, George allowed writers to come and stay in his bookshop, where thirteen beds were hidden in amongst the shelves, and it became known as the Tumbleweed Hotel. His only demand was that those who stayed pen their autobiography on a sheet of paper, and give it to him before leaving. George claimed that as many as 40,000 people, including writers of the Beat generation like Allen Ginsberg and William S. Burroughs, slept in the shop over the years.

His daughter Sylvia – named after Sylvia Beach – is now using some of these autobiographies to put together a book on the history of the bookshop. 'The Tumbleweed biographies are wonderful,' she confirms.

'They're an oral history of the shop, and a fascinating social account of young people travelling through Paris. Most of them are filled with literary aspirations and romantic dreams; it's touching to see how similar a twenty-one-year-old staying in 1972 is to one staying today. We continue this tradition and right now we are housing a French environmentalist writer, a Polish poet and an English actor. Over Christmas we usually have some regular Tumbleweeds who return. This year there was a Polish-English actress, a Cambridge student of Arabic, and an Israeli girl studying mathematics whose father also stayed at the same time. It definitely feels like an extended family, which is what my father used to tell me when I complained about being an only child.'

Much like his bookshop, George Whitman was eccentric. He had a terrible temper, read a book every night, and often shoved bank notes inside books behind the desk for safe keeping. Instead of trimming his hair, he'd burn the ends off using a candle, and he once threw a book out of a window at a customer because he thought they might enjoy reading it. The actor Owen Wilson was once in Paris filming Woody Allen's *Midnight in Paris*, and decided to venture upstairs at Shakespeare and Company in the hope of meeting George, who lived above the shop and at that time was spending most of his days in bed. George apparently glanced up, nonplussed: 'Have you written a book?' he enquired. 'No', said Owen. George tutted, unimpressed, and went back to reading his book. He ruled his bookshop like a slightly dishevelled monarch, and everyone loved him for it. He died in December 2011 at the age of ninety-eight.

I first visited Shakespeare and Company after George's death, where it's now run by his daughter Sylvia. The poetry section is my favourite part of the shop: a little alcove sectioned off by a garden gate. There's also a piano, and a Wishing Well, and 'The Mirror of Love' upstairs, where hundreds of notes have been left by customers. Notes haven't just been put here, though – I picked up a copy of John Green and David Levithan's *Will Grayson, Will Grayson*, and out of it fell a handwritten message from another customer: *'Hello, fellow nerdfighter. You have good taste.'* This made me smile from ear to ear.

At the start of 2014, I had a chat with Sylvia, who has now been running the shop for the past nine years, and we talked about Shakespeare and Company's plans for the future:

'In the early 2000s, I picked up a guide book on Paris and read the paragraph on Shakespeare and Company,' Sylvia told me. 'To my dismay, it said we were "resting on our laurels".

'I had just started working at the bookshop, my father was in his late eighties and struggling to run the shop in the way he used to, and it's true that the stock and events were pretty poor. It was difficult for him to pass on the reins of his "rag and bone shop of the heart," partly because it had been his life for over fifty years, and he ran it in his own, very unique way. I turned out to be equally stubborn, and there were moments when customers had to witness a family row over the installation of a telephone, or how to organise a section. These usually ended in laughter, and I hope my father would be happy with all the changes I've made now, including our sporadic literary festivals. I have always tried to respect the original idea, just polish the edges.

'When I take a little distance, I think the history just gives myself and the team I work with inspiration. Sylvia Beach was a dynamic and most wonderful, dedicated bookseller. My father had a unique way of running his shop which can be encapsulated in some of his sayings:

1. Be kind to strangers lest they be angels in disguise.
2. We wish our guests to enter with the feeling they have inherited a book-lined apartment on the Seine which is all the more delightful because they share it with others.
3. How he described the bookshop: Where the streets of the world meet the avenues of the mind.

'Like a literary Chelsea Hotel, I just want to expand on all the ideas that George put in place: a literary crossroads – Paris is ideal for that – where you can find a place to sleep, spend hours reading in the library, sip on good coffee in our new (upcoming) café, and watch an event, which could be a concert with Moriarty, a film screening with Vincent Moon, or Margaret Drabble reading from her latest novel.

'I'm not sure what my favourite part of the shop is. It could be the Wishing Well or the Mirror of Love. What I miss greatly when I am not there is the vibrant, electric energy the shop holds. For whatever reason, it definitely has a very strong spirit that is energising. I remember two French geographers who strolled into the bookshop and suddenly stopped still. *"C'est incroyable!"* they exclaimed. Apparently there was a strong current of water rushing under the bookshop, and they said this gave a very particular energy to the place. I don't know if that's true but there is something, in the shadow of Notre-Dame and on the banks of the Seine, that continues to draw people to this place.'

❖ BOOKISH FACT

For the last thirteen years of his life,
Casanova was a librarian.

• A CHAT WITH CLAIRE KING •

Claire King is a British novelist. After university she spent twenty years working anywhere in business that allowed her to tell stories, before finally realising what she wanted to be when she grew up. Her debut novel *The Night Rainbow* was published in 2013. She lives in southern France with her husband and their two daughters, happily ever after.

" I moved to France with my husband nearly fourteen years ago. The plan was to live cheaper, work less and create some space in our lives for having children, as well as the other things that were then evading us – like my desperate urge to write. We settled on a tiny hamlet in the foothills of the Eastern Pyrenees, buying a crumbling wreck of a house and set about bringing our imagined future to life.

Hidden down one of the pink marble backstreets off Perpignan's main Place de la République, amongst the wrought-iron balconies of city-centre apartments, the pavement cafés, the *charcuteries* and *chocolatiers*, is a tiny specialist bookshop called Bédé en Bulles.

I was lost when I found it. The streets around the Place de la République are labyrinthal and narrow, and the buildings tall and tight, affording no view of helpful landmarks for those of us who are less than brilliant navigators. It's not the kind of bookshop I ordinarily would have entered had I been in the UK. Bédé en Bulles sells exclusively *bandes dessinées*, or *BD*, a cross between comics and graphic novels – the colourful realm of Asterix and Obélix, of Tintin and the Smurfs and a circus of other characters who enjoy relative obscurity beyond francophone borders. But I did go in that day, partly out of bookshop curiosity, partly on a hunch and partly because I could employ the perfectly conceivable pretence with my two young daughters that I hadn't been lost at all, but had been intending to take them to a bookshop all along.

In fact, we rarely visit bookshops here in France. It's curious to dwell on that statement, because for a book-loving English expat like me bookshops are definitely something you miss. But we live far from the kind of big city that might support a foreign-language section in a bookshop, and although we do visit the local library our family has never made the switch to French books. It is a language issue, but not in the way you might think. We are all pretty competent in French. Both my daughters were born here, and are essentially bilingual. They switch between speaking or reading French and English seamlessly, which never fails to impress me. But we are still an English family, and whilst French is our neighbourhood language, and that of the workplace or school, it's one in which extra effort is required both to understand others and to express ourselves. English is the familiar – the comforting language of home. This naturally means that when we read for pleasure we all lean towards books written in English. That isn't such a problem for my husband and me, but it became apparent that if the girls were to keep up and blend in with their friends at school they would need other avenues of exposure to French. And I was reluctant to turn on the TV.

So we found ourselves in a tiny backstreet bookshop in Perpignan, which reminded me for all the world of the record shops I spent hours browsing in as a teenager. The walls are covered in posters, and the books – exclusively hardbacks – are stacked in racks like LPs and, as in a record shop, classified broadly by genre, then by author (separated by handwritten cardboard dividers), and finally alphabetically by title. Unlike books displayed on a row of shelves, it's impossible to browse only by looking: you are forced to engage with the books, flipping through cover by cover. In an age where we are becoming more accustomed to web pages and clicks, there is something magically tactile about choosing a rack where something catches your eye, delving deeper into the books with your fingers and then coming back up and out and down again until the one perfect book has been chosen. This is a shop that insists you touch the books.

On that first visit I told the girls they could choose one book each, and off they went, flicking through the racks. Stories involving horses were pulled out for my approval, followed by little vampires, mischievous brothers and sisters, gobs of green goo and explosions of sweets. Familiar characters were rejected in favour of the new and exciting. Books were examined and replaced, and occasionally – when they found a good one – held on to and read on the spot.

Although she was excited by many of the books' covers, at the time my youngest daughter was only four, and I doubted we would find anything there to suit her. It's not easy to read a comic strip aloud to a child, since the artwork is an essential part of the narration, and she wasn't reading fluently by then. But I was wrong. She discovered a series of pantomime comics, featuring *Petit Poilu* (Hairy Little Thing) whose fantastical adventures to other lands are so beautifully drawn that over the course of the 180 or so images in each album, she herself could narrate the tale. There is a great power in this type of book. It calls upon the imagination of the reader, who must interpret expressions, empathise with the characters and invent the dialogue.

For my older daughter it was a treasure trove. She delighted in finding bubbles of dialogue which are not the 'correct' French that she learns at school, but the 'real' French she encounters in the playground. Her *BD* books have given her precious access, in a safe context, to the slang words and abbreviations used by other children but never at home or amongst adults. This contemporary French has given her more confidence amongst her peers, and she has taken great pleasure learning expressions that her parents don't know…

Finding this bookshop, and its world of *Bandes Dessinées*, was a triumph. Now, whenever we go back, the girls are able to tell

the owner what they have enjoyed, and he recommends new series and authors that they might also like. It has also helped me
understand more about how we engage with language and with
stories, how we combine the two, and has reminded me
that, for children and adults alike, learning to enjoy
books is not always synonymous with learning to read. **"**

✶ ✶ ✶ SOME WONDERFUL THINGS ✶ ✶ ✶

◆ Le Bal des Ardents in Lyon frames its doorway with a huge archway made entirely out of books.

◆ In the town of Auvers-sur-Oise you can find an old rusty mail train that's now a second-hand bookshop.

◆ La Infinito bookshop-café in Madrid is open from early morning until late at night. Filled with books, cake, music and art, it hosts musical brunches, Japanese bookbinding classes and even a School of Storytelling.

◆ One of the oldest antiquarian bookshops in Spain is Librería Bardón, founded in 1947 by Luis Lopez Bardon, and now run by his son Luis Bardon Mesa, who started working there at the age of fourteen. The rooms are filled with beautiful leather and gilt books, and chandeliers hang from the ceiling.

◆ Lello Bookstore in Porto, Portugal is widely considered to be the most beautiful purpose-built bookshop in the world. It was designed by Xavier Esteves and its neo-Gothic interior has a double staircase, dark wooden galleries and stained glass ceilings.

◆ Ler Devagar in Portugal translates as 'Read Slowly.' You can find it inside the LX Factory, which was built in 1864 to make threads and fabrics. Now the factory is used as a creative space that incorporates this bookshop as well as design workshops and art galleries. As it used to be a factory the ceilings are extremely high, which makes the fact that the shelves stretch from the floor right up to the ceiling all the more impressive.

♦ The Bertrand Bookstore in Lisbon is the oldest bookshop in the world still trading. It opened in 1732, and is now the heart of the Bertrand bookstore chain, which has more than fifty shops. The original location of the bookshop was destroyed in an earthquake, but it has been in its current location since 1755.

♦ Librairie ptyx in Ixelles, Belgium, calls itself a house for thought. The biographies of famous writers are inscribed across the white-painted exterior.

♦ In 2009 a woman called Aurelie ran a bookshop-caravan called L'Esprit Vagabond, and travelled around Mellois in France. She sold books and told stories to those who didn't have an independent bookshop nearby.

• A CHAT WITH JOANNE HARRIS •

Joanne Harris is the author of the Whitbread-shortlisted *Chocolat*, and many other bestselling novels. She was born in a sweet shop, plays bass guitar in a band first formed when she was 16, and is currently studying Old Norse. She lives with her husband and daughter in Yorkshire, about fifteen miles from the place she was born.

" I grew up in Yorkshire, but my mother was French, and that's what we spoke at home. I read in both languages as a child. I read adventure stories and Jules Verne, Ray Bradbury and Edgar Rice Burroughs – all sorts of things. I also read things that had been translated into French without realising it. Until quite late on, I thought that Agatha Christie was French because my grandfather had a large collection of her books. As he didn't speak English, it didn't occur to me that the books I was reading were initially written in that language. It's not something you think about as a child; you just get lost in the story. I didn't visit bookshops until I was older. We didn't have one in Barnsley, but we had a library and I went there a lot. I bought some books through my school, as well; most of my children's books came from there – but not the French ones (those were given to me by relatives).

I still very much like the bookshops on Cecil Court in London, places like Goldsboro Books and also the antiquarian bookshops there, too. I always find it especially lovely when a bookshop like Marchpane, which specialises in old editions of *Alice in Wonderland*, is run by someone who not only sells books but is also a passionate collector themselves. Someone who has a real feel for the books, and appreciates their beautiful illustrations. I've done some great book swaps in Marchpane – an old edition of *Gormenghast* for some illustrated copies of *Alice*. I love to go there.

I think the enthusiasm and passion of bookshop staff is what will keep bookshops going in the future: you can't replicate that online. The bookshops I know that are doing really well are the ones who have knowledgeable staff, aren't afraid to organise events, and know their clientele. These are the bookshops that use their space for more than just selling, and the bookshop therefore becomes a destination for customers, not just a means to an end. Anyone can sell books, and anyone can buy books online: good bookselling is all about making the buying of books an experience.

If I could open up a bookshop of my own, I think I'd open one dedicated to illustrated books. Story books, and fairy tales in particular. Things that I used to love as a child. I had some wonderful books of myths and poetry when I was little, and I remember how much I loved them. I'd want to open the bookshop in a place where there aren't any other bookshops. I've been to a number of African countries where books are in such short supply, and the wonder of books is still very much present. It would be a pleasure to open a bookshop in a place where people are not yet jaded, and don't take books for granted. **"**

◆

Montolieu

Near Carcassonne, surrounded by vineyards, there's a little village called Montolieu. Here, back in the day, they used to make paper. In 1989 Michel Braibant, a local bookbinder, decided to resurrect Montolieu's history, moving his bookbinding business there and enouraging others in the field to do the same, in the hope of creating a French Hay-on-Wye. Richard Booth even bought a building there to support the project, and now many second-hand booksellers, artists, printers and craftsmen have come together to bring Montolieu's love of literature back to life.

❖

BOOKISH FACT

Jiří Mahen Library in the Czech Republic
has teamed up with an advertisement
agency to cover the outside of local trams
with paintings of bookshelves.

Customers can use the wi-fi in these
trams to sample library books, in the hope
that they'll then travel to the library later
and take a look at the books themselves.

Belgium

◆

Brussels

Brussels has many amazing bookshops, all within reach of one other. In the centre of the city, tucked inside an old shopping arcade from the 1840s called the Galeries Royales Saint-Hubert, you can find Tropismes. A huge, mirrored dance hall now filled up with books, it was once the home of a famous 1960s jazz club, the Blue Note. Down the road there's another gallery from the 1800s, the Bortier Gallery, also full of books, but this time mostly stalls, alternating between selling books and art. Ten minutes further down the road, at the Belgian Centre for Comic Strip Art, is Slumberland bookshop, full to the brim with comic books.

Brussels is also home to Cook & Book – a real concept bookshop. You can even dine there, from a menu selected from the cookbooks they sell. Books hang down from the ceiling on strings; the English section has been designed to look like a gentlemen's club, and in another part of the shop there's a book room designed to look like an American-style diner, with a real car parked in the middle of the floor.

◆

Redu

Rural Redu, in the middle of the Ardennes forest, became the Book Town of Belgium thanks to the efforts of Noel Anselot, a journalist who also worked in the oil industry. In the 1970s he bought a house there with his family, and wrote a cookbook. Then a visit to Hay-on-Wye gave him the idea of creating his own Book Town back home, and he started by opening a bookshop on a converted snail farm. At Easter in 1984 booksellers and book lovers – some 15,000 of them – came from all over Belgium to set up stalls, and Anselot hosted Richard Booth to declare Redu and Hay-on-Wye formally twinned. Several of that weekend's visitors ended up staying for good to set up their own bookshops. There are now more than twenty, including an English bookshop called the Crazy Castle, and Henriette Luyckx's dedicated to books about the sea. There's also a paper-making workshop and an engraving studio.

Spain

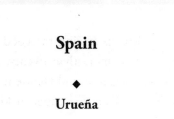

Urueña

Urueña is an old medieval village near the Cantabrian mountains with only a few hundred inhabitants. On top of a hill, and surrounded by the walls of its castle, it has several churches and a museum displaying church bells from the fifteenth century. It has also become the first Book Village of Spain.

There are twelve secondhand and antiquarian bookshops in Urueña, amongst them the Wine Museum Cellar Bookshop; the El 7 Bookshop, which sells books on bullfighting; Alcuino Caligrafía, where you can take courses on calligraphy; and the Artisan Book-Binding Workshop of Urueña. The village also has a permanent exhibition called 'Between the Lines: A History of Books'.

❖

BOOKISH FACT

On 10 May 1933, in Bebelplatz in the centre of Berlin, the Nazis burned more than 20,000 books. Nowadays the sculpture of an empty library stands in the square, created by Micha Ullman and large enough to contain every one of the books burned. A plaque there quotes Heinrich Heine: 'Where they burn books, they will also burn people.'

Portugal

◆

Tell A Story, Portugal

'Once upon a time there was a country born with the gift of writing, an author that wanted to tell a story, a book that wanted to be read, a tourist who did not speak Portuguese and a bookshop that did not know how to remain in the same place.

All of them joined together and wrote a new story.'

Tell A Story is an organisation that sets out to promote Portuguese literature, by selling English translations of its works to British tourists from a bookshop van that tours the country. They believe that nothing makes a person want to travel to a place more than to read about it, and their hope is to inspire people to return. The Tell A Story van also sells pens, paper and postcards, for travellers to write down their own tales and send them to their friends, and foster a chain-reaction of storytelling. There is even a 'Writers' Font,' which you can download from their website. They created the font by copying and merging the handwriting of famous authors, to encourage others to follow in their footsteps.

∗ ∗ ∗ SOME WONDERFUL THINGS ∗ ∗ ∗

◆ In 1929 Frau Schoeller opened Marga Schoeller Books in Berlin, specialising in European Literature and drama. Despite refusing to sell Nazi literature she managed to keep the bookshop open after Hitler had come to power, and even secretly sold books banned by the regime, which she kept hidden in the basement.

◆ Librairie La Fontaine in Lausanne, Switzerland, has been designed with five rings of bookcases, each of which encloses a white-padded reading-room, to offer the reader a safe 'reading cave' for peaceful browsing.

◆ In Bassano del Grappa in Italy is the beautiful Libreria Palazzo Roberti, a bookshop in an eighteenth century palazzo split over three floors, with grand frescos by Giovanni Scajaro, a student of Gianbattista Tiepolo, which hosts regular classical concerts and photography exhibitions.

◆ 10 Corso Como in Milan, in a converted industrial building, is not just a bookshop but a bar, café and hotel, as well as one of the city's hippest boutiques, with décor that switches from exotic plants to state-of-the-art furniture. Founded in 1990 by the publisher Carla Sozzani, sister of *Vogue* Italia's editor-in-chief, it has been followed by branches in Seoul and Tokyo.

◆ Libreria Acqua Alta in Venice is a haphazard second-hand bookshop that has so many books they've made a staircase out of them. There are bath tubs filled with books, several bookshop cats, and a gondola in the middle of the shop also full to the brim with texts of all shapes and sizes. Once you've found a book amidst all the chaos, there's a seat by an open door looking out over Venice's canals where you can put your feet up and relax.

◆ Tvedestrand, by the south coast of Norway, is one of its country's Book Towns, with small white houses filled with books. It also has a hotel which the President of the International Organisation of Book Towns considers the best bookish hotel in the world. (There is another in Fjærland: see page 139).

❖

BOOKISH FACT

More books are published in Iceland per
head of population than anywhere else in
the world.

Iceland also pops up in many books and
films, such as Jules Verne's *Journey to the
Centre of the Earth*, when Professor
Lidenbrock and his crew disappear down
Snæfellsjökul. Its capital is home to the
Sagas of the Icelanders and Poetic Edda,
landmarks of world literature, and, as
such, Reykjavik offers many literary tours
of their city.

The Netherlands

◆

Amsterdam

The biggest book beast in Amsterdam is The American Book Center. It has a wall of books twelve metres high alongside the central staircase, an Espresso Book Machine that can print out self-published and out-of-copyright books within minutes, and a regular 'Pitch Your Book to a Professional Publisher' event. There's also a Waterstones in the centre of town which, weirdly, sells Marmite and Branston Pickle.

But the city is particularly well supplied with specialist bookshops, too. It's almost as though a bookshop came along, split up its sections and spread itself out all across the city, enabling one to bounce off another: one for architecture; one for comics; one for fashion and photography; one for art (Boekie Woekie); one for literary magazines, and a specialist Anne Frank bookshop at the Anne Frank Museum. Next to the Oudemanhuispoort, a covered passage with many small second-hand bookstalls, is Perdu (French for 'lost'), the poetry bookshop, which links with the university to hold an event every Friday in the theatre next door – which used to be a hospital kitchen. Speakers, writers and philosophers come from all over Europe to give talks here.

◆

Selexyz Dominicanen, Maastricht

Selexyz Dominicanen was opened in Maastricht a few years ago in a converted thirteenth-century Gothic Church by the bookshop chain Polare. When Polare went bankrupt in 2014 local book-lovers raised money by crowd-funding to keep this one beautiful bookshop open. They raised 200% of the money they needed to survive, and rather than simply asking for donations, customers were asked to become 'Friends of the Bookshop' by investing in the business for an annual return of 5%.

◆

Waanders in de Broeren, Zwolle

Waanders in de Broeren, opened in 2013, was a similar concept to the shop above: turning a fifteenth-century Dominican church into a beautiful bookshop. Waanders has been a publishing house since 1836, and their new bookshop in Zwolle was established to commemorate Wim Waanders' fifty years of running the company. The architects were required to redesign the 550-year-old Gothic interior around its original stained-glass windows and pipe organ, which is still used for concerts.

Finland

◆

Arkadia Bookshop, Helsinki

Ian Bourgeot had collected so many books in his house over the years that he decided to open his own shop. That was in 2008, and since then Arkadia Bookshop has become a vital part of the local community, hosting over 700 events in recent years. The shop is so large that four events can be happening at once without disturbing one another. Ian doesn't host all of them, but allows authors and various groups to use the space – the more the merrier. There are concerts and film screenings, restaurant days and art exhibitions, and lectures on the origin of the universe. There is space to browse and read, and areas to simply sit and think. Arkadia also has a chapel, a piano, a pool table, a bookshop dog called Lola, and even a bookshop snake, too: a handsome boa constrictor by the name of Ziggy. (Don't worry: he's in his own enclosure, not slithering along the shelves.)

Sweden

◆

Larry's Corner, Stockholm

Larry's Corner looks as though the owner, Larry Farber, has opened his house to the public and started selling things from it. That's because he loves everything he sells, and can tell you a story about every object. He has a projector in the shop which he uses to show films in the evenings, and offers customers coffee from his makeshift kitchen behind the counter. Larry says everyone who has the good sense to walk through his front door is a friend.

'I'm from Detroit,' Larry told me, 'but I've lived here in Sweden since 1980.'

'I got my Swedish library degree in 1986 and worked as a librarian in a small Swedish city until 2000. I loved the job but I hated the co-workers, so I went nuts and two friends I opened up Nitanaldi, my first store, named after one of the first vamps in Hollywood. After the first few months, the other two jumped ship and left me running the place. We specialised in pretty much all obscure culture – books, films, music, art toys.

'When I met my second wife, Barbara, she didn't want to live in a small town in Sweden, so I moved to Stockholm and renamed the store Larry's Corner. I am kind of an expert at weirdness, so thought I would concentrate at selling everything I find interesting – out-of-print obscurities, comics and old records – losing my ass at it but having fun. I tend to drive customers crazy being so in love with it all, but I love what I do.'

◆

Mellösa

In the small Book Town of Mellösa, one of the bookshops can be found inside a house. All of the books there have been arranged by colour: a room of blue books, another of red, a third of green. In the kitchen they sell cookery books.

Norway

◆

Fjærland Book Town

Fjærland translates as 'spring land,' and it's definitely in the spring that the town comes to life. Situated near the Jostedalsbreen, the largest glacier in mainland Europe, it could easily find a home in Philip Pullman's *His Dark Materials* trilogy: during the winter, with up to six feet of snow and temperatures as low as -20ºC, its bookshops become what the locals call deep-frozen. The Book Town is officially closed then, but those who live there wrap up warm and zoom around on kick-sleds, shipping in books and piling them up ready for the warmer weather. The Honesty Bookshop, a stand-alone bookcase at the side of the road with a money box attached, was blown down in last winter's extreme weather.

Fjærland became a Book Town in 1995, with support from Richard Booth, and has a mere three miles' worth of bookshelves. Straumsvågs Antikvariat is one of the largest shops. The curation of the place is what makes it special, the idea being to preserve old structures, so you can find bookshops in abandoned buildings everywhere, from ferry waiting-rooms to stables, from banks to grocery shops, and even cowsheds and pigpens. Books are sold in the Hotel Mundal, too, a rather eccentric place that opened in the late 1800s, and whose staff hand-wove all of its rugs, carpets and hangings.

❖

BOOKISH FACT

The biggest collection of books in the world, before the invention of the printing press, was the great library of Alexandria, founded by Ptolemy Soter in 283 BC, and thought to have contained half a million books. Books were often stolen from libraries as trophies of war, and every ship that came into the port of Alexandria was raided by officials, who confiscated any books on board. These were then taken to the library, where copies were made; the library kept the originals, and gave the copies back to the ship's crew.

Denmark

◆

Torup Eco-Village

Økosamfundet Dyssekilde is the oldest eco-village in Denmark, formed in the 1990s on a potato field. It's since extended into Torup, which had been a village since the eleventh century but by the twenty-first was largely abandoned. Now, however, people have moved back. The aim is to be as self-sufficient as possible, and to create a community that is vegetarian, spiritual and humane. To this end the villagers only own the exact plot of land their house is built on, so there are no fences or walls, and the whole village can therefore be used as a playground by the children who live there.

An essential part of a peaceful, spiritual environment, the founders of Økosamfundet Dyssekilde decided, was books and storytelling, and they've set up many self-service open-air bookstalls and honesty bookshops around the village. You can find them inside a garage, a workman's hut, a disused stable, a farm entrance and a restored railway station. They've also established the Nordic Book Festival, and been recognised as Denmark's National Book Town.

Germany

• A CHAT WITH CORNELIA FUNKE •

Cornelia Funke was born in 1958 in the German town of Dorsten. As a child she wanted to become an astronaut or a pilot, but then decided to study teaching at the University of Hamburg. After a spell as a social worker she had a stint illustrating books, but soon began writing her own stories. Her international breakthrough came with the fantasy novel *Dragon Rider* (1996), which stayed on the *New York Times* Bestseller list for seventy-eight weeks. She is also the author of *The Thief Lord*, and the award-winning Inkheart trilogy.

“I grew up in a small town in Germany, longing for adventure and the promise of a bigger world. Books gave me all that. They were my windows and doors to the world. There were two bookshops I went to in my home town (apart from countless visits to the local libraries, as otherwise I would have ruined my parents!). One of them, Buchhandlung König, is still in existence, and each time I visit my parents I offer to sign books there to support it.

I think the first book I ever bought with my own money was a non-fiction book: Robin Lane Fox's *Alexander the Great*. I was obsessed with Alexander – I could even explain the strategy of his battles – and it was quite an expensive book, but it felt like bringing home treasure.

I've noticed that, whichever country you're in, independent bookstores are magical places. I wouldn't like to say I have favourites, as I can think of many stores I found enchanting whose names I forgot. In the US there are such wonderful ones as Book Soup in Hollywood, in Los Angeles where I now live; Books of Wonder in New York; Anderson's in Naperville; Hicklebee's in San Jose. In London there are of course the Daunt bookshops on Marylebone High Street and in Hampstead. There is the Mainstreet Trading

Company in St Boswells, Scotland, and Topping & Company in Bath. Sadly the owners of my favourite neighbourhood bookstore, Portrait of a Bookstore, retired. It was right within my favourite café in LA, so it was coffee and books, a magical combination.

Today books for me mean looking at the world, learning about it, seeing it through the eyes of others. They are a brilliant device for shape-shifting, as we can slip into the skin of authors from other times, other cultural backgrounds, brilliant minds who give us a new perspective on life and the world – something we all need from time to time. Books give us the unique chance to talk to the dead, listen to their stories, use their words as a time machine, a flying carpet to faraway lands. Books make time and space meaningless; they give us witty and wise companions; they teach us that our worries and fears are shared by others – and they give us words for what we sometimes cannot express.

We all order books online by now, but that only gives us the books we know about. The bookstore delivers a completely different thrill: we can find printed treasures we hadn't heard about. We can touch and open and taste words between the pages, discover, fall in love... A bookstore offers a much more sensual encounter with books. It reminds us of all the life that is hidden within them. And when we find a book in a beautiful bookstore it adds to it the memory of a place and time, which I find a wonderful extra to have for any book on one's shelves. As for taking children to a beautiful bookstore – no other place can make them realise better that books rhyme with adventure, with treasure, with discovery. What better start for a reading life? If we want them to fall in love with books, this love has to start in a bookstore.

If I opened my own bookshop? Heavens, what a tempting scenario! I would open it either in Los Angeles, as that is my home, or in Salisbury, which is one of my favourite places in Britain. Or maybe I would open it in the middle of a forest and make it a very mysterious and adventurous place, a destination for book pilgrims! I would have figurines of my favourite book heroes between the shelves, both writers and literary characters. I would have copies of original manuscript pages, letters from one writer to another, objects that remind readers of famous books, to be found all over the store, sometimes hidden, sometimes in plain sight. I would have shelves at the right height for children and books you can only get to on a ladder. I would have a flying carpet to sit and read on, and a cave, and a tree house. As for the books: I would of course have children's books, but also fantasy and science fiction, the classics, my favourite books, books on plants and animals, travel guides, mythology... you can see it would be a messy bookstore, a shop you could really lose yourself in. And of course it would have a silver-framed mirror. **"**

◆

Berlin Story, Berlin

The Berlin Story calls itself a life-size history lesson. It's the only bookshop completely dedicated to selling books about the city, with 5,000 titles in twelve different languages, ranging from history books about Prussian kings to detective novels set just down the road. It's run by Wieland Giebel, a film producer, and is now linked with the Historiale Berlin Museum.

◆

Hugendubel, Stuttgart

Hugendubel is one of the most successful bookshops in Germany, managed by the fifth generation of the children of Heinrich Hugendubel. Outside the flagship store in Stuttgart are television screens showing customers reading; inside are what they call 'Reading Islands,' massive leather chairs and huge carpeted cubes where you can sit down and examine a book or five.

◆

TASCHEN, Cologne

Set up in 1980 by Benedikt Taschen, TASCHEN is a comic book and art publisher that has bookshops in twelve major cities around the world, and is known for its lavish production standards and sometimes controversial material. My favourite book of theirs is a history of the American travelling circus by Linda Granfield and Dominique Jando, a beast of a book in a beautiful slipcase weighing in at 5 kg, which almost made me collapse carrying it home. This is nothing compared to *SUMO* by Helmut Newton, a limited edition that weighed 30 kg and which TASCHEN sold for a staggering $15,000 apiece.

◆

Wünsdorf Book Town

Wünsdorf is a slightly odd place: a military base since before the First World War, after the Second World War it became the headquarters of the Soviet military in East Germany. Fifty thousand soldiers lived there, and it was cut-off from the outside world like a gated community, with its own bakers, schools, theatre and hospital. So when the Soviet army left in 1994, Wünsdorf became a ghost town, full of empty buildings, broken pianos, run-down bunkers and old army uniforms, as well as plenty of ammunition and boxed-up chemicals to be disposed of. It's been dubbed the 'Forest City'. A few of the buildings have since been converted back into houses, and a local group runs a museum about the history of the town, with tours of the many abandoned bunkers, but with a statue of Lenin still standing in the middle of it all, lichen climbing all over him, it remains an eerie setting.

In 1998, to try and piece together Wünsdorf's many untold stories, its residents decided to turn it into Germany's first, and so far only, Book Town. Several derelict buildings have been reclaimed by bookshops, with one called the Bunker Shop specialising in military history, and another that features a small Russian tea room.

❖

BOOKISH FACT

There are all manner of strange bookshop-hybrids in the world. In Rhodes in Greece you can find the Lindos Lending Library, run by an American lady called Sheila. It's not just a library: it's also a launderette!

Greece

The two main bookshops in Athens are Βιβλιοπωλείο Ευριπίδης (Euripides) and βιβλιοπωλεία Ελευθερουδάκη (Eleftheroudakis). Euripides, with four floors and a lending library in its café, is named after its founder, Euripides Prince, and describes itself as a 'lodge' where book-lovers can come and relax. The Eleftheroudakis chain has been around since 1918, and is still run by the Eleftheroudakis family. Indeed, the Greeks have a saying when it comes to books: 'I was told only the Eleftheroudakis would be able to find it.'

◆

Atlantis Books, Santorini

In 2004, Oxford students Craig Walzer and his friend Oliver were on holiday on the island of Santorini, got drunk, and decided to open a bookshop. Despite niggling doubts once they were sober again, after graduating they recruited a couple more friends, bought second-hand books from as many places as they could, filled up a van, and drove back to Santorini, where they opened Atlantis Books.

'We've got beds hiding in among the bookshelves, and we light bonfires on the terrace in the evenings,' says Craig.

'We have friends far-flung across various continents, and the bookshop has been a meeting place for all of us. So many crazy things have happened over the years: we've even starred in Chinese soap operas. This Chinese film crew had arranged to come and shoot in our shop, and they said they'd turn up at two in the afternoon, but then I got a phone call from their production assistant at eight in the morning saying that everyone was outside and could they come in? So, I walked outside in my boxers straight into the middle of a scene they were filming.

'We produce handmade books in our back room, and we're running a festival this summer with authors from all over the place. We'll have some Greek writers visiting, a thirteen-piece brass band from Bulgaria, and a concert pianist from Carnegie Hall. We'll also have chefs, making us food. And, to top it off, two of our bookshop's founders will be getting married in the middle of it all.'

✳ ✳ ✳ SOME WONDERFUL THINGS ✳ ✳ ✳

◆ Vilnius University in Lithuania has a campus bookshop called Littera, which looks more like a church than a bookshop. It has dark wooden shelves and low, sweeping ceilings painted with frescos. It's beautiful enough to distract you from the books themselves.

◆ Bokin in Reykjavik, Iceland, is so full of second-hand books they've had to start piling them up at the end of the aisles, and around the counter. You can't really see in through the windows, either, because… they're covered up by books. When the legendary chess player Bobby Fischer moved to Iceland, Bokin apparently became his favourite place. He said it reminded him of bookshops back in New York, and he'd spend so much time there reading he'd often fall asleep.

◆ Akateeminen Kirjakauppa (The Academic Bookstore) in Helsinki, Finland, opened in 1969, but is part of a company that has been selling non-fiction since 1893. The store is lit by geometric glass skylights shaped like open books.

◆ Denizler Kitabevi in Istanbul, Turkey, is a beautiful bookshop on two floors specialising in old maps of the world. They have even started printing map reproductions, and publish books on history and navigation.

◆ The Haymon Bookstore in Innsbruck, Austria, looks like something from outer space. The shelves are matt black, and dimly-lit, making the books displayed on them look like stars floating in the night sky. As the ceiling is a mirror, that bookish sky appears to go on forever.

◆ Írók Boltja, which translates as 'Writers' Bookshop', has been selling books in Budapest, Hungary for sixty years. It took over the premises of a café that was one of the most famous places in Hungary at the beginning of the twentieth century for artists and writers to gather. Írók Boltja intends its tea room to continue the tradition; meanwhile its mission is to spread the word about great Hungarian literature.

◆ Ezop Antikvarijat in Osijek, Croatia, don't just sell antiquarian books but also rare postcards from all over the world. Their Siamese bookshop cat is called Luna.

❖

Bookish Fact

Antonio La Cava, a retired teacher from Ferrandine in Italy, promotes reading with his Bibliomotocarro, a motorbike-based house of books. It even has a roof and a little chimney.

He travels around the villages of Basilicata in the mountains of southern Italy, lending books to children who don't have libraries nearby. When he pulls into village squares the Bibliomotocarro starts playing organ music to let people know he's there. Antonio also has a notebook in which children can write their own stories. The children in the first village he visits start a story, then the children in the next pick it up, and so it goes on. The next time the Bibliomotocarro comes round, the children get to read the whole story they helped create.

Italy

◆

Montereggio

Montereggio is a small village on a hill in southern Italy, placed at the heart of bookselling legend. During the sixteenth century the men of Montereggio embarked on a new occupation: selling books. They took an oath and ate a hearty meal before they set out each summer, because they knew their journey was going to be a long one. They came to be known as the Shepherd Booksellers – but these were booksellers who could not read.

First, they travelled to towns in the north, where they sold chestnuts and cheese to publishers in exchange for books they no longer wanted. Whilst the Shepherd Booksellers couldn't read the books they were buying, they could recognise those that were well-made. When their bags were full, they'd hoist them onto their backs and head back to the countryside, where, so the legend goes, they'd sell their books to the farmers, who couldn't read either. The booksellers would recite passages they'd learnt by heart, assuring the farmers that these were very important books they should definitely own. It's no wonder that, back in the day, travelling booksellers had a bit of a reputation for being rather sneaky.

However, over the centuries many booksellers from Montereggio did learn to read and left the village to join the publishing firms in the towns; some even went further afield and opened bookshops in Spain and France, and one, a Signor Maucci, went aboard a ship as a cabin boy in 1850 with 180 books and sailed to Argentina to open a bookshop. Altogether, 150 descendants of those original Shepherd Booksellers are said to be running bookshops across the world. These days the roads leading into the village are named after famous Italian publishers, and Montereggio has become a Book Town.

Estonia

◆

Slothrop's, Tallinn

Slothrop's is Tallinn's first second-hand English bookshop, run by London designer Lewis McGuffie and his American friends John and Scott. Lewis had come to Tallinn on an artist residency, and fell in love with the city. He lived with John in an artist project space called Ptarmigan, where they met Scott, who had lived in Estonia for nearly ten years. The shop was Scott's idea; years before he'd bought some 900 books with the intention of opening one, but hadn't found the time.

'None of us had much experience in bookselling,' says Lewis, 'but we were all avid readers. John's vision was for a cultural space where we'd have events and sell books by local authors, artists and designers. Scott, being a bit older and more grounded, simply wanted to sell books and make money. At first I was just happy to have a bookshop. What has kept me going is making the place look good – it's been a vanity project of sorts. It's nice to imagine oneself as a bookshop owner: I'd even thought I might wear more tweed and drink a little whisky while pondering the Greek classics – I was quite motivated by these sort of clichés. And there's no better chat up line than, 'Want to come see my bookshop?'

'It's all gone to plan in that we're still open. We're still trying to figure out what our long-term prospects are – we imagine ourselves in a much bigger place, incorporating a café or even a co-working space like Beta-Haus in Berlin: Tallinn has a strong start-up culture that's heavily integrated with the social scene, so combining a specialist bookshop with an opportunity for freelancers to work in a nice environment makes sense. We had to move a year after opening, and managed to strike up a deal with the Writers' Union of Estonia, who own the space we're in now, and we sell some things for them.

'With the exception of the summer months most of our customers are locals – and not just the Estonians, who are often more keen to read in

English from a young age, but the Russian-Estonians. It's a young community around the shop – generally under thirty-five: English was only taught, or even permitted, from 1991, after the end of Soviet rule.

'Some of the regulars are pretty interesting. For example, there's an old Scottish guy who has a Russian wife and teaches English and is in the habit of bringing his own dried fish with him wherever he goes. He's been politely reminded by the bar staff more than once that he shouldn't when I've gone for a pint with him – he brought some to the shop once, too, but I was fine with it because he gave me a few.

'A very old guy who was a bookbinder had seen us on Estonian television, and brought with him as a donation two books he had restored and re-bound years ago. We talked in broken English and a little Estonian; it was simply a kind gesture and he wanted us to keep them. The two books were German-Estonian dictionaries printed in 1873; we still have them, and our research suggests they could be quite valuable.

'Recently we bought about 600 books from a private collection in Washington DC, and they were amazing. A lot of interesting history, covering everything from China to Native Americans to the Jewish diaspora, as well as a lot of antiquarian books. It was fascinating going through them and getting an idea of who the owner was and what interested him. We found quite a few old notes and postcards left over in them, too. By the end it felt quite profoundly personal and a joy to have seen such a collection. All the stuff we find we keep and pin up on a wall in the shop. It's turning into quite a gallery of pictures, hand-written notes, old bus tickets, flyers and photographs.

'Finding great books is a real treat. Looking for a book on the Silk Road and discovering a travelogue from 1953 of some French guys who drove from the Balkans to Kashmir is a very analogue experience, and this is why I think bookshops are important. They offer a tangible experience of human creativity.'

❖

BOOKISH FACT

Vladimir Nabokov wasn't just a writer:
he also collected butterflies. Whilst
travelling in the US in the 1950s, he
scribbled down the details of the butterflies
he caught on index cards. At the end
of each day he turned those index cards
over and wrote his novel *Lolita* on the
other side.

Russia

◆

Dodo Magic Bookroom, Moscow

Shashi Martynova is a Russian translator and one of six avid readers and publishing professionals who have owned and run Dodo Magic Bookroom for the last five years. She's put what she calls her 'whole life energy' into the world of books, believing in the power of the word to educate as well as entertain, and wants to ensure that books cross language barriers to reach as many people as possible, to make them laugh as well as free their minds – to which end Dodo have published the only book in the Russian language on Monty Python. 'It all began fifteen years ago,' says Shashi, 'when I first prepared a very thick encyclopedia for print. Some people in Russia say it's quite difficult to get into the publishing industry, but once you're in, it's impossible to get out again. It captures you somehow.

'So my friends set up a publishing house, and I happily ran it for them for six years. However, in 2009, I felt as though I really needed to go to the other side – the post-production side. I wanted to see what happened there. I couldn't shake the image and history of Shakespeare and Company out of my brain, and Magma Books too. I had to do it myself. There is also something about Lewis Carroll that encouraged me to make the change. There are so many different translations and illustrated editions of *Alice* in Russia – pretty much all of my generation grew up on it – he's got a bit of a cult here in Russia, and a huge artistic following. Something about escape, new worlds and crazy imagination. So I wanted to create a bookshop somewhat in its image. The Dodo in our name is from *Alice in Wonderland*, and it's also a joke about the book industry in general – paperback books very much live on, though, despite what others might say.

'My plan was to open a type of bookshop that doesn't really exist in Russia: a non-serious, but playfully profound, bookshop. Because

Russians are generally damn-serious people; you can't really fool around being Russian. Yet we wanted to try because, after all, reading is like a fun drug – only safe, legal and cheap!

'So that's what we did. We started off as one bookshop, and now we've got five: we've opened one a year across the city since starting. Each bookshop is pretty tiny, about eighty square metres, and not more than 10,000 books. We call our bookshops places where you can buy fairy tales for any age: Tolkien, C. S. Lewis and Gaiman, and pretty much anything legendary from world literature, stories with a twist, anything picturesque and weird.

'One of our bookshops is inside a cinema, and there we have books on screenplays and visual art. Another one is in a huge cultural centre for children, so there we have more books on parenting and children's arts and crafts, and then we have two small bookshops within department stores, to spread the name of our brand and help keep our other stores open.

'We manage to enjoy ourselves, and survive, and every other month we get requests to franchise our business. I'm very wary of this, though: I am very protective, and proud, of our name, and I don't think we can recreate the exact kind of experience we have without overseeing everything, and I can't split myself into lots of different people and run around our – huge – country. And imagine the cost! We do a lot of educational work: lectures and seminars on anything from literary studies to theory of communication, and we do city games, too – quests based on literature. This works really well with our customers, especially with teenagers.

'Bookselling is not about money: we need money to keep doing it, but it's not our driving force, not our passion. Post-Soviet publishing and bookselling is only twenty-three years old here, so to be five years old is really cool to us. Our passion is in the word, the power of the word, its freedom and the ability of stories to take us to other places. To live many lives at once, as mindful reading allows.'

Africa

❖

Bookish Fact

Kenya National Library started its Camel Library Service in the 1990s to promote literacy in nomadic communities. Three 'Camel Caravans', each consisting of three camels, operate in the north-eastern part of the country, reaching settlements near Garissa Town and Wajir. Each 'caravan' carries 200 books and travels with a librarian, two librarian assistants and a camel herdsman. Those who borrow books can keep them for two weeks, until the camels come round again.

Kenya

◆

Kinda, Kibera

When Khaleb Omondi's father died in 1992 he had to drop out of college and move to Kibera, the largest slum in Nairobi, to live with his uncle. He found work in the city cleaning offices, and in the afternoons he'd set up a stall and sell things by the railway tracks. In Kibera there was a sacred feeling around books, he realized: education was almost a sacred concept. He brought out his old school books to see if they would sell, and despite the people of Kibera having hardly any money, they bought them: they wanted their children to learn. Khaleb bought more books to sell, and then borrowed some money from friends to open a small bookshop in Kibera, and ran it with his wife. He called it Kinda, a Lou dialect word for 'endeavour'. Sales went well, so he started to stock new books, too.

Following the 2007 election, when Mwai Kibaki was made president, an outburst of terrible violence in Kibera saw over a thousand people killed, and hundreds of thousands flee their homes as gangs moved through the slum destroying buildings. Khaleb's bookshop was looted and destroyed, and while running away from the violence he was hit by a car, which broke his leg and left him in a cast for nearly a year.

Not one to give up, Khaleb eventually recovered to set up a new bookshop a short distance away in Magiwa, whilst he set about restoring his Kinda bookshop. He didn't have any money to buy books, but his suppliers helped by giving him stock on credit. Though in constant fear of further attacks, Khaleb is determined to keep going. His second bookshop is called Jo Kinda: 'people who endeavour to succeed'.

✴ ✴ ✴ SOME WONDERFUL THINGS ✴ ✴ ✴

◆ J. K. Stores Books in Machakos, Kenya doesn't just sell books. In the spirit of diversifying and luring people in with other wares, it also sell cows.

◆ If Fahmi Iskander Fahmi, who runs the Marawi Bookshop in Sudan's capital Khartoum, thinks you're someone who properly appreciates books, he'll take you to its stock room a few streets away. Hidden in an alcove, behind a metal door, and down some steps, you'll come upon an underground book warehouse with a million titles.

◆ The Aboudy Bookstore and nearby Aboudi Bookstore in Luxor, Egypt, are run by a family of Egyptologists who have been bookselling since 1909. The two branches are run by cousins, and specialise in books on Egyptian history, as well as selling papyrus paintings. The Aboudy branch's bookshop cat goes by the name of Pussy Cat.

◆ David Jacob Amunabi has called his four bookshops in Nairobi, Kenya 'Bingwa' Bookshops: 'bingwa' meaning 'hero', as he believes that education and books can transform and empower his customers.

◆ Adams and Company was set up in South Africa in 1865 to sell stationery, magazines and books to the colonial community. It's grown over the years to eight branches across the country, selling textbooks to students, teachers and nurses.

◆ Kerry-Leigh Snel opened the Book Boutique in Amanzimtoti, South Africa. 'There's nothing quite like sitting on a couch surrounded by books,' she says: '. . . essentially sharing a room with the thoughts of extraordinary people from the past and present. We really get close to our customers, and they feel like part of the family. Some have donated book-related decor, such as a Paddington Bear, and a painted plate with a bookshop theme.

'I think bookshops remind people that we need to slow down – to stop and appreciate other human beings, read about other people's lives, about new discoveries and past misadventures. There are no gender or age restrictions in bookshops, just a whole lot of soul.'

Tanzania

◆

TPH Bookshop, Dar es Salaam

At TPH Bookshop they're keen advocates of progressive thinking and freedom of speech, and do as much as they can to help locals get into reading, as well as making regular book donations to local orphanages. I talked to booksellers Walter and Mkuki about their shop and its history.

Walter told me: 'TPH Bookshop has been part of a colourful and progressive history of Tanzania and, indeed, many would say of Africa since 1966 when it was founded. Throughout the years when Tanzania hosted liberation movements from southern Africa, the bookshop – then part of Tanzania Publishing House – was the meeting-place of revolutionary intellectuals, writers, poets and active freedom fighters. In 1973 TPH published Walter Rodney's seminal work of African history, *How Europe Under-developed Africa*. That really put us on the world map.'

Mkuki added: 'What makes us unique is that, unlike other bookshops which only stock text books or imported books in English, we sell a lot of local publications for both children and adults, and have the biggest selection of local Tanzanian and Africa-wide books. Our favorite books are children's books, and we have a lot of them in Swahili for the local market, since they are very hard to find. Tanzania is a majority Swahili-speaking country, so it is important to make sure there are books that children can read in their own language in order to help instil a reading culture at an early age. Since the beginning we have held on to the belief that we must make sure people have a diverse range of literature to read so that we can develop a literary culture. The bookshop has become a kind of community centre, too. We are very proud of this, and are working hard to ensure we keep a constantly updated catalogue and keep our customers engaged.'

South Africa

♦

Ike's Books, Durban

Joseph David Mayet, known as Ike, was the son of a South African paraffin salesman. Born in 1926, he spent three years in hospital as a child with a bone infection called osteomyelitis. To make his days more bearable he lost himself in books, stories of all kinds, and made a promise to himself that one day he would open a bookshop.

Forty-three years later, retired from his day job making boilers, he set about keeping that promise. He studied bookbinding and helped restore rare books in the Gandhi Library, and in 1988 he opened Ike's Bookshop in Durban, selling a huge range of books, including titles that were banned. Thirteen years later, when he decided to retire, his friends took the bookshop on, and it was officially reopened by J.M. Coetzee. Ike passed away a year later, in 2002, since when writers have signed the walls of the bookshop in his honour.

♦

Book Lounge, Cape Town

It was Mervyn Sloman's five-year-old twins who gave him a pep talk over breakfast about opening an independent bookshop. He'd been working for a chain bookstore, after leaving work in IT:

'I'm generally terrible at taking advice from others,' he told me, 'but faced with two five-year-olds over the breakfast table, each armed with a spoonful of milky cereal, I would have agreed to anything. Thankfully, their advice was mostly sensible. As for their excitement at the prospect of us hosting a story time every Saturday morning for kids, all I can tell you is that our children's books manager, Verushka, has been running Story Time every Saturday morning since we opened. My kids are now eleven going on sixteen, and their advice keeps on coming.

'I spent the first eight months of 2007 looking for a possible venue without any luck, and had pretty much given up on opening a shop that year, when my wife came home one day in September and announced she'd found the perfect spot. I went down the next morning to find a beautiful Victorian building in a part of town that was allegedly in the first throes of regeneration – though evidence of that was patchy, to put it mildly. The ground floor on street level was a beautiful space, but too small for what I was looking for. When I got access to the building, though, I found a hole in the floor through which I could see an underground basement that had never been used for anything except collecting mould. I immediately fell in love with the possibilities of the space and began what turned out to be nightmarish negotiations. I eventually signed a lease in the last week of September, and then had to oversee the building site that it quickly became in order to turn everything around so we could open the bookshop on the first of December.'

In 2013 the Book Lounge and Cape Town's Central Library tried for a world record by knocking over 2,586 books in a row – they await Guinness approval. Meryvn has also been running his literary festival Open Book alongside the bookshop for the past three years. It aims to give Cape Town a truly international literature festival, to bring the best of South African reading to an international audience, and to do all it can to promote a love of reading among the city's youth. Last year saw the creation of Pulp Fiction, an art installation made out of 25,000 novels that were due to be pulped. At the end of the festival Mervyn sent out invitations to libraries and other organisations in need of reading material, asking them to come and take away as many books as they could carry. The shop also runs a library appeal, asking customers to buy books in store to be sent to schools in need of them.

'Eight months after opening, we won an award for the Best Independent Bookshop in South Africa,' Mervyn says, 'and of course, in the best tradition of self-promotion, we shared the news with our mailing list. What followed was a flood of congratulatory emails from our customers, many thanking us for the impact we had had on their lives in those short eight months. I sat at my desk crying. I will always be grateful for the generosity of spirit evidenced in the positive feedback that we receive from our customers. I love my job. What's not to love? A life without stories is no life at all.'

◆

Quagga Books, Stellenbosch and Kalk Bay

George Curtis started one of Quagga Books' two antiquarian bookshops in South Africa about twenty years ago; his son Simon owns the other. 'My dad's shop is in Kalk Bay, an area known for quirkiness and antiques,' says Simon. 'I think it is safe to say it has become one of the landmark shops of the area.

'Then, about eight years ago, I was changing careers and moving from Cape Town to Stellenbosch: this presented a good opportunity to expand the business. I soon learned that the best things about running a bookshop are: the people I get to meet, the books I get to hunt down and buy, being my own boss and not being too stressed about things in general. The worst things are: the people I get to meet, the rubbish some people expect me to buy, being my own boss and being stressed about everything.

'One of the main challenges in South Africa is sourcing good stock, and for the Stellenbosch shop we can draw on a far wider pool of all the surrounding towns and farmlands, which also brings us into contact with many Afrikaans buyers and sellers. At the moment we have a small section called "Strange Books", books on things like suicide, drugs, occult, folklore and other odd subjects. The glass cabinets in our shops are always a favourite – they house our more valuable books, arranged with things like baboon skulls and tortoise shells. Because of the type of books we deal in, it is the object that is important. We mostly sell out-of-print books but also beautifully bound early editions of books still in print. Our bookshops are not so much places to meet, as many other bookshops are: more places to find inspiration.'

North America

❖

BOOKISH FACT

Sean Ohlenkamp and a team of twenty-seven volunteers stayed up all night for several nights to make an intricate video called 'The Joy of Books,' a short stop-motion film in which the books of Type Bookshop in Toronto run around in the dark. They arranged the books by colour, made them look like piano keys playing, and got the books on Fred Astaire and Ginger Rogers to dance with one another. (Not to mention that every morning they had to make sure all the books were back in the right place before opening time!). You can find their video on YouTube.

• A CHAT WITH ANDREW KAUFMAN •

Andrew Kaufman is the author of *All My Friends are Superheroes*, *The Tiny Wife* and *Born Weird*. He also makes films, and lives in Toronto.

" When I was in my second year of university, I fell in love with Second Look Books in downtown Kitchener, an industrial town in Southern Ontario. It was a used bookstore, and in 1988 downtown Kitchener wasn't really a safe place to be. There was a Hell's Angels clubhouse around the corner, lots of sketchy people doing sketchy things. To get to this bookstore I had to take a bus, then walk past bikers and drug dealers and drunks. When I opened the door and stepped inside Second Look, it really was like entering a different world. At the same time I was discovering Vonnegut and Salinger and Brautigan – three writers who remain on my all-time favourites list. For some reason Second Look always had copies of these writers' books when no other used bookstore in the city did. So even though going there was a little scary, it had to be done. I've fallen in love with a lot of bookstores since, but because of the time and the place and the journey, there was a magic to Second Look that I doubt I'll ever feel again. **"**

Canada

◆

The Monkey's Paw, Toronto

When you walk into a bookshop, you know immediately if it's your kind of place. Because its curation is so intrinsically linked with the person who owns it, it's also possible to gauge whether you'd like to sit down with them, buy them a coffee and listen to their life story – which you know will be peppered with bookish references, strange customer stories and an overall sense of love for what they do. The Monkey's Paw is my kind of bookshop, and Stephen Fowler, who owns it, is my kind of person.

The bookshop houses the Biblio-Mat: the world's first random antiquarian book-vending machine. Insert $2 and, as it says on the front, 'Every book a surprise. No two alike. Collect all 112 million titles.' Being presented by books in this way forces the customer to really look at the title and engage with it. Similarly the book displays in the shop show contrasting titles next to one another; mixing up subjects so that a customer can't scan the titles in a blur. Each book stands alone and gets to be judged for what it is.

'I don't remember a time when I didn't love books,' Stephen told me.

'I was a wistful only child, and I grew up in a house with a lot of books in it, so it seemed inevitable that I would become a bookworm. Most of my parents' books were from the mid-twentieth century, but they had also inherited a few shelves of leather-bound antiquarian titles from some forgotten ancestor. While the other neighbourhood kids were outside playing football I lay on the living-room floor, trying to decode the roman numeral dates in those leather books.

'I grew up in Kansas City, Missouri, not a place renowned for its bookshops, and my main access to books, other than from my parents' shelves, was actually libraries. I always took enormous pleasure in haunting the stacks, and finding shelves that nobody else ever looked at. In high school, I would find old Jules Verne novels, or First World War combat memoirs, and marvel at the dates on check-out cards in the pockets – nobody had checked out those books for decades! The librarians were probably baffled, but perhaps also charmed, that some teenager in 1980 actually gave a damn about such books.

'I didn't really discover bookshops until I was in my twenties, living in San Francisco. I had a room-mate who was a certifiable bibliomaniac, and naturally he worked at a second-hand bookshop. It seemed like a job I'd be well-suited for, so I convinced him to hook me up with another shop that was looking for a part-time clerk. That first job was at Albatross Books, in the Tenderloin district of San Francisco. And once I entered that world, there was no turning back. I started visiting bookshops everywhere I went – not exactly compulsively, but always with a strong nagging sense of curiosity.

'For the initial inspiration for the Monkey's Paw – the seed crystal of the idea – I must credit an eccentric bookshop clerk named David Park. He gave me my initial training in the book trade, from my very first day working with him at Albatross Books. It was a huge store, occupying three floors, and down in the spooky basement David had created a section he labelled "Floop." This was a bizarre and sundry assortment of books that could fit into no other section – the oddballs and ugly ducklings. I used to look for excuses to go 'work' in the basement, so that I could sit on the floor in front of the Floop section, and browse the weird books. I found it by far the most interesting and inspired section in the store. I wish I could remember more examples of the books I found there, but I distinctly recall an old hardcover copy of Dingwall's *Girdle of Chastity*, utterly defaced with an obsessive crazy person's marginalia; also a cheerful book on Scandinavian family saunas, with lots of pictures of naked blonde people. It was a rich trove indeed, and awakened me to the fascinating possibilities of "odd" and "overlooked" books as a category unto themselves.

'Adobe Bookshop, and its co-founder Andrew McKinley, had a profound influence on me, too, because Adobe was the first hip second-hand bookshop I'd ever encountered. Throughout the twentieth century there had always been famously hip bookshops selling new books: Shakespeare & Company in Paris, City Lights in San Francisco, St. Mark's Books in New York – places where the fashionable intellectuals of the day hung out. But traditionally second-hand bookshops didn't have that level of glamour: they were either just repositories of old paper bric-a-brac, very earnest suppliers of academic material, or exclusive antiquarian joints reserved for rich collectors. Adobe broke the mould because the clientele was cool and contemporary, but the material was all second-hand. It became a destination for young, hip weirdos, a place where louche grad students from Berkeley hung around discussing German philosophers and film theory.

'I loved Un Regarde Moderne in Paris, which I discovered in the 1990s – a bookshop devoted exclusively to visual culture. Kayo Books in San Francisco had an amazing aesthetic celebration of the oddball, the garish, the sleazy. In the midst of all the lurid paperbacks, they had a "Weird Nonfiction" section. I also have to credit Bill Bilby, owner of Chelsea Books, with two other important lessons: first, his shop was always tidy and thoughtfully-organized – a remarkable trait in secondhand shops; and second, he was visibly enthusiastic about his stock. He was the first bookseller I knew to describe a book-artefact as "sexy"! A cynic might denigrate this latter trait as a mere sales tactic – because indeed his infectious enthusiasm successfully sold lots of books – but the fact is that the guy was, and is, just a completely mad bibliophile, and being in his shop with him, listening to him effuse about his books, and watching the way he would stroke them and savour them, was profound. It made me realize that we in the trade are actually evangelists of bibliophilia, and embracing and spreading that passion is the only way to ensure our survival.

'The nature of the stock at my own bookshop, the Monkey's Paw, is (to quote our publicity materials) "Diverse twentieth-century printed matter, with special emphasis on visual culture; obsolete opinions and technologies; lesser-known works on highly specific topics; books as artefacts; and pop detritus", and that hasn't really changed much since

I opened the shop in 2006. Of course the beauty of a second-hand bookshop is that, while they might be the same flavour of books, the individual titles are always different. Many visitors to the shop will never see the same book twice.

'Friends of mine – probably concerned by the worn-out state of my clothes – have suggested that I could wring more money out of the business by specialising in more truly rare and valuable books. But that's not likely to happen either. I don't particularly enjoy selling books to rich people; I prefer to sell books to regular human beings, who buy the sorts of unexpected books I could imagine buying for myself. Truly valuable books – the $5,000 signed first edition of some literary landmark, or the eighteenth-century ornithology folio with glorious hand-tinted plates – are already-acknowledged commodities in a high-end collectors' marketplace. I prefer making the discovery myself, finding forgotten curiosities like a 1930s guide to running a beauty salon, or a pamphlet offering advice to Vietnam-era draft-dodgers – something I can dig up in a flea market in Indiana and sell in Toronto to an enthusiastic book-geek for $20. That's the stuff that gets me out of bed in the morning.

'The Biblio-Mat was originally conceived as a fun way to recirculate a variety of kind of curious but essentially unsaleable old books that had piled up in the basement. As a promotional stunt it has vastly exceeded my expectations, and for the last year I've had to buy a whole separate stock of books specifically to keep the thing fed – not first-rate books, but still sufficiently old and interesting to meet my criteria (pre-1980, hardcover, mostly obscure non-fiction).

'From a conceptual standpoint though, the Biblio-Mat is really just an extension of the shop's philosophy. We try to offer customers the experience of bibliographic surprise and discovery. We stock books that most people aren't likely to have seen before – ideally books they can't believe even exist. In our front window, and on our various face-out displays inside, we try to exhibit maximum cultural diversity, even dissonance. So you'll see a psychiatric manual on sex crimes next to a collection of Hungarian fairy tales, next to a book on Maoist communal farming, next to a field guide to mushrooms. And quite often, someone who didn't realize he had any interest in Maoist communal farming ends up buying the book.

'The same principle applies when you put $2 into a vending machine, and a surprise book falls out. It's a trivial amount of money to risk – a single Canadian 'toonie' – and you end up with a printed artefact you've never heard of before, on a subject you may never have even considered. The technology of manufacturing plywood, or the memoirs of a nineteenth-century minister in rural New Zealand, might be books you'd never pull down from a shelf; but hold one in your hand, and approach it with an open mind, and you'll likely find something worth reflecting on. Many of the books that come out of the Biblio-Mat are genuinely interesting, and in other cases their very banality makes them remarkable.

'Far and away the most notable Biblio-Mat customer is a man named Vincent Lui, who bought one book a week from the machine for all of 2013. He read every book – no matter what the title or subject – from cover to cover, and wrote a review of each on his blog (therandombookmachine.com). Obviously Vincent takes the prize for most fanatical devotion to the Biblio-Mat, and his commitment is on-going: though he himself no longer reviews a book a week, he has now opened up his blog to submissions from the public, and plans to maintain the thing indefinitely.

'The experience of finding a viable niche for a bookshop at a time when so many others are going out of business has certainly been validating. It has confirmed that my taste in peculiar old books, and my desire to match them with customers, is not completely delusional. I wouldn't say that running the Monkey's Paw has changed my personality, but it has definitely made me a bit more confident about the worthiness of my own predilections.'

> " A good bookshop shows you the books that you never knew you wanted. It doesn't merely fulfil your desires, it expands them. If you know the book you want, go into a bookshop and buy it, you have failed. "

Mark Forsyth, author of the *Sunday Times* #1 Bestseller *The Etymologicon* and its sequels.
blog.inkyfool.com

A BOOK-LOVER'S THOUGHTS ON WHY BOOKSHOPS ARE IMPORTANT

Kerry Clare talks about Book City in Toronto.

" I heard it on the radio that my local bookshop was going to close. I was washing the dishes and listening to the news, and there it was. I hadn't seen it coming. I went into the other room, still holding a dish. I said, 'Book City is closing. What are we going to do?'

Though I should have seen it coming. In our city, bookshop closures happen every other week, but I'd figured my neighbourhood was immune. I'd taken for granted the pleasure of picking up a novel while having popped out for a carton of milk. We were cloistered in a bubble, I thought, where economic rules did not apply. The most terrific throwback: a book would occur to me, and I could walk up the street to get it. It was instant gratification; the universe at my fingertips.

But it was more than that. (More than the universe? *I know!*) More than just access to books as a commodity, Book City was a destination, an atmosphere, and it was people. It was the first place I'd ventured to after each of my babies were born, hobbling along the sidewalk clutching my C-section incision. It had been our final trick-or-treating stop last Halloween. It's where I do all my Christmas shopping, and buy gifts for everybody's birthday. Where I'd pre-ordered the new Donna Tartt, the new Zadie Smith, their on-sale dates momentous occasions.

It's where we wander to on lazy Saturdays for somewhere to be. Where I wandered during those terrible months of new motherhood, the shop staff the bright spots in my life. So many purchases because these same people were savvy enough to display the right books at the till, and the conversations we'd have during our transactions. The joy of running into other bookish friends there, all of us vibrant in our natural habitat, surrounded by books. And the confidence that the obscure small-press volume of poetry I absolutely needed this instant would definitely be found on their impeccably curated shelves.

So there I was with my dish, and I started to cry. The grief was huge and real, which was ridiculous because one must maintain some sense of proportion, but then the amazing thing was that, as news of Book City's closure travelled, other people understood. I wrote about it on my blog and on Twitter, and people got in touch to say that they were sorry, to tell the sad stories of when they'd lost their own local bookshops. And while it's terrifying to consider a world without bookshops, it's heartening to realise so many people still know how much we're losing when they're lost.

The full price of books, for me, has always seemed a fair exchange for the privilege of an excellent independent bookshop in my neighbourhood. Books cost money because they are items of value, and I think that in our hunger for deals and discounts we have forgotten what value is. Of course, part of this is sentimental, which is what they call it when I despair about the loss of things that make me happy, but it is also practical: where will I buy my books now? **99**

Kerry Clare reads and writes in Toronto. She blogs about books and reading at her blog, PickleMeThis.com. Book City has since re-opened one of its branches in Toronto – not Kerry's local, but one not too far away. Hopefully this is a sign of things to come...

◆

Munro's, Victoria

In 1963 Jim Munro and his first wife, the author Alice Munro, opened a bookshop in a narrow space near Victoria's movie theatres. Now you can find Munro's in a neo-classical building designed for the Royal Bank of

Canada in 1909. The building had been modernised in the 1950s, but when Munro's took it on in 1984 they set about returning it to its former glory, and the restoration has received two heritage awards. The bank's basement vaults are now used as the storeroom. In 2013, the bookshop celebrated fifty years with a black and white ball and much champagne, and a month later Alice Munro won the Nobel Prize for Literature.

'Walking out of a store with a stack of new books for the night-table is always a delight,' says Munro's manager Jessica Walker:

'You see, bookshops are information centres – they seem to be a place where people can ask all sorts of questions, questions you would never ask in a shoe shop! We actually have an ongoing series of journals, a sort of collective store memoir, called "Tales too Terrible to Tell." I believe we are on volume six or seven now. All the good stuff, plus all the dumb questions, goes in those books. Though we've also formed strong friendships with customers, too, and there are even some who regularly bring us chocolate!'

◆

The World's Smallest Bookstore

A hundred miles outside of Toronto, between Kinmount and Salerno Lake, by the side of the road, there's a ten-foot-by-ten-foot cabin which calls itself the World's Smallest Bookstore. All the books are $3, and there's an honesty box to pay. When you leave, you take with you a hand-out entitled 'Why I love books'. The reasons listed include: 'Books do not interrupt'; 'Books never require medical attention'; and 'Books do not demand TLC... but they tend to get it anyway.'

◆

Re: Reading, Toronto

Christopher Sheedy had a dream of owning his own bookshop for over twenty years before starting Re: Reading books in Toronto.

Atlantis Books, Santorini, Greece.

Fjærland Book Town, Norway.

Khaleb Omondi at his bookshop Jo Kinda, Kenya.

The world's first antiquarian book-vending machine: The Biblio-Mat at
Monkey's Paw, Toronto, Canada.

Munro's Books, Victoria, Canada.

Singing Wind Bookshop, Arizona.

© Greg Alford

John K. King Used & Rare Books, Detroit – inside an old glove factory.

© FTG Designs

El Ateneo Grand Splendid, Buenos Aires, Argentina.

© Ryan Poole

Luis Soriano and his Biblioburro, Colombia.

Bookseller in Calcutta, India.

APODON in Xiamen, China.

KID'S REPUBLIC in Beijing, China.

© SAKO Architects

The Bookworm, Beijing, China.

BooksActually, Singapore.

D's Books, Phnom Penh, Cambodia.

Numabookcat, Tokyo, Japan.

© NAM + numabooks

'When I moved to Toronto in 1986, at the age of twenty, I was poor, says Christopher. 'I mean, new-pair-of-socks-was-cause-for-celebration poor. I was also a voracious reader, and having to choose between dinner and a new book was tough. You see, bookshops are dreams built of wood and paper. They are time travel and escape and knowledge and power. They are simply put, the best of places.

'It was in Toronto that I discovered the wonderfulness of used bookstores. I grew up in a small town that didn't have any, so this was new to me. Queen Street West at that time had several used bookstores, used record shops and a few comic shops as well. This allowed me to feed my habit and I always thought, "I would love to own one of these places and just work there all the time." I filed the dream away, though, and hoped to do it once I retired.

'Flash forward some twenty years and I had a wife, a house, a cottage and a career. The only problem was, as happy as I was in my life, I was not happy in my job. Working for someone else had always rubbed me the wrong way, and my then boss was a Champion Rub-The-Wrong-Wayer! So I was determined to find a new job, and hopefully a better boss.

'Then the most amazing thing happened. My wife, Joanne, a woman I have known since we were seven years old, said, "What happens if your next boss is an Olympic Level Moron? What if you get the top job but your Board of Directors are a bunch of Award Winning Meddlers?" My response was, "Well, what are my options?"

'This next part just goes to prove how well she knows me and exemplifies why I love her. She said: "What about the bookstore? You were planning on doing it when you retire: why not look into doing it now?"

'Me: "....."

'Joanne: "There are forty-plus bookstores in Toronto: if they can do it, I know you can too."

'See why I love her?

'So in November of 2008 I set about learning how to open the bookstore and what it would take to make it a success. I had spent a great deal of time in used bookstores as a customer over the years and so I felt I had a pretty good understanding of how they worked. I talked to several owners in town who, once they learned I was not planning on opening near them, were very helpful with the details. It took me November and December to learn enough so that I felt I really had a shot at doing this. So, on 4 January 2009, after spending a snowy, windy day on the Danforth to gauge foot traffic in bad weather months, we finalised our decision: I was opening a bookstore!

'Next step: to resign. This was a wonderful bit of joy. To walk up to my boss and tell him that 12th February would be my last day was a giggle-inducing event. The look on his face was priceless. It turned out that my last day at work was also the day they gave us the keys to our premises. I had a bookstore! (Well, actually, I had an empty store which we needed to fill with books!) We hadn't boarded up the window, so people could see in while we did it up. Not only were people peering into the store to see what we were up to but I could also see who my customers were going to be. Namely, families with strollers and a slew of dog owners out for their walk. This resulted in a sign in the window saying dogs were welcome, and designing my aisles so that even a double stroller could make it to the back of the store (know your customers!).

'Many things have happened in the five years we have been open: an article in the *Toronto Star* on the front page of their Business Section; many online reviews; and winning Critic's Pick for Best Bookstore in Toronto from *NOW* magazine (not best used bookstore: *best bookstore*). My favourite author, Robert A. Heinlein, once wrote: "Happiness lies in being privileged to work hard for long hours in doing whatever you think is worth doing." He was right. There is no feeling in the world like finding that one book you have been looking for for years. What comes close though, is being the guy who helped them find it. I am a lucky, lucky man.'

" Is there anything better than entering a secondhand bookshop? Inexpensive books (good!), but also books you've never heard of, or barely heard of, by people who were writing in your genre, and your target age-category, just a generation or even half a generation ago, and have already been either completely or half-forgotten. There they are, in hardback and paperback, remembered. Honoured. Which, since we nearly all end up there eventually – let's not pretend – honours us all. "

Cliff Mc Nish started writing a story about a witch for his daughter when she was ten, and then promptly forgot about her until it was finished. This became *The Doomspell*. *The Times* describes him as 'one of our most talented thriller writers'. He is also the author of *The Hunting Ground* and *Breathe*.

❖

Bookish Fact

In 1905 the Book Wagon appeared in
Maryland, with shelves attached to its
exterior, drawn by two horses, delivering
books to houses far out of town. A few
years later, Minnesota had the first
bookmobile you could actually walk in to.
In 1917 the Bookshop Caravan was
brought to life by two female booksellers in
Boston. Inspired by Christopher Morley's
Parnassus on Wheels, a novella about a
travelling bookstore, Bertha Mahony, who
ran the Bookshop for Boys and Girls,
rolled up her sleeves, planned her journey,
and set off on a tour of the east coast,
selling books as she went. Publishers paid
for the Caravan's upkeep and petrol, and
Christopher Morley declared himself the
Caravan's godfather.

• A CHAT WITH REBECCA MAKKAI •

Rebecca Makkai is the author of *The Borrower* and *The Hundred-Year House*. Her work has appeared four times in *The Best American Short Stories*, and regularly in *Harper's*, *Tin House*, and *Ploughshares*. The recipient of a 2014 NEA Fellowship, she lives and teaches in Chicago.

" I spent six hours as a bookseller this fall, and was just proud, by the end, to have done minimal damage. I sold books at two Chicago stores, Lake Forest Book Store and City Lit Books, as part of Indies First, an event launched by the writer Sherman Alexi in which writers hand-sell at independent bookstores on the Saturday after Thanksgiving. The idea is that customers will be drawn into the stores to chat with local writers – a plan that probably works far better if you're Sherman Alexi than if you are, like me, a writer only one customer between the two stores had ever heard of, basically just a crazy lady getting in their faces to recommend books.

Let me say: I am not cut out for this work. I would offer to help a customer, listen to what he wanted, run off to grab the *perfect* book – if he likes music, he would love this novel about jazz in the thirties! – and watch as he subtly ditched it for a coffee-table book about horses. And I tried too hard to sell short story collections: the publishing world thinks stories don't sell but, I figured, that's just because they're not *trying* hard enough! Time and again, the customer would wince at the jacket and say, 'Oh, I only read novels.' In the same way she might have said, 'Oh, raccoon meat is not for me.'

And here's why I couldn't do this for a living: each time, I was deeply hurt. Sure, I can write a novel – but can I sell someone Paris Hilton's autobiography without a look of horror and betrayal on my face? I'm not that strong. "

USA

◆

Old Inlet Bookshop, Homer, Alaska

The Old Inlet Bookshop, run by Andrew and Sally Wills, is also home to the Mermaid Café and the Mermaid B&B, where you can rent a room, sit in an outdoor hot tub, relax and look out at the bay and the mountains. Andrew says that his dad got him, his grandfather and his mum all involved in the book trade. His mum has owned the Lord Randall Bookshop in Massachusetts since the early seventies; he grew up working in her shop.

Andrew moved to Alaska in 1982 and fished commercially for a living. 'I started the bookshop in 1997 because it was safer than crab fishing in the Bering Sea in the winter,' he says, 'and because the Kenai Peninsula was infested with the Spruce bark beetle, which was killing all the old growth spruce trees. I started helping a buddy with his sawmill to salvage the trees and make them into lumber. After I built my house, I started building bookshelves. Soon after that, I opened my shop. I may be the furthest-west bookshop on the road system in mainland USA. I know there is a bookshop in Nome, Alaska, but you can't drive there unless it's by dogsled!'

◆

Brazenhead Books, New York

Brazenhead Books is a rather controversial bookshop in New York City. It doesn't have a business card; it doesn't have a known address. It is a secret bookshop. Pushed off the streets of New York by a hike in rent, owner Michael Seidenberg reinvented his second-hand bookshop by moving it into an apartment. Because of where it is, it's now a speakeasy-esque bookshop. If you want to visit it, you have to email or phone Michael to arrange a time to stop by. Whatever your opinions on its legality, there's something adventurous about having to track down a secret bookshop that, technically, doesn't exist.

◆

Tattered Cover, Denver

In 1971 a small bookshop opened in Cherry Creek, Denver. Three years later it went on the market and was bought by Joyce Meskis. Joyce is one of the strongest voices in independent bookselling in America. She's won awards for intellectual freedom, including the American Library Association Award for Free Expression and the Author's Guild of America Award for Distinguished Service to the Literary Community. She's also the director of the Publishing Institute at the University of Denver. In other words, she knows what she's talking about.

'My first bookselling job was in 1960,' Joyce says. 'That was during a period of my life when I was in college and found myself needing to supplement my income to help pay my tuition bills. When I graduated, I moved from the mid-west to Denver and started graduate school there, and I was still working in bookshops and libraries, working out what I wanted to do with my life. I literally woke up one morning and thought, "You idiot – don't you realise you've been doing what you love all these years? Why don't you just get on with it!" So, that's what I did.'

In Joyce's first eight years of running Tattered Cover, the 950-square-foot bookshop expanded seven times into adjoining retail space. There are now three branches, one in a converted theatre, which they call their 'theatre of ideas', as well as a stall in a local airport, and soon they'll be opening a small satellite shop in a railway station, too. They have three coffee shops, have gone from two employees to 150, and do 500–600 events a year, hosting authors such as Margaret Atwood, J. K. Rowling, Bill Clinton and Barack Obama. 'We're forty-three years old as a company,' says Joyce, 'but I like to think we're more than a company: we're part of the city.' For all the expansion, though, it's the simple things she continues to love about her job. 'When a child comes up to a bookshelf, catching sight of a favourite book, their face lights up. I still get a thrill with that.

'Once we had an event with the astronaut John Glenn, who was the first American to orbit the earth. I was sent a note from the son of one of our customers – the boy's name was Duncan, and he'd written a letter for John Glenn: he said he couldn't come to the event because it was past his bedtime, but that he really wanted a signed copy of his book. He also said he wanted to be like John when he grew up. It was such a sweet letter, and I'm sure John was touched by it. To think that, as a bookshop, we can bring people together like that (via letter or in person!) is just lovely.'

◆

Powell's, Portland

Powell's actually began in Chicago, when Michael Powell opened his first bookstore in 1970. He'd borrowed $3,000 to acquire the lease, and the bookshop took off so successfully that he was able to repay the loan in just two months.

Powell's was taken to Portland by Michael's father, Walter, a retired painter, who'd spent a few months working in his son's bookshop the previous summer. In Portland he opened his own bookshop called Powell's, causing controversy by stocking hardbacks, paperbacks, old *and* new books all mixed together on the same shelves. The controversy worked, though: they now have six bookstores, and are considered one of the best bookshops in America.

◆

Uppercase Bookshop, Snohomish, Washington

Leah McNatt and the folk of Uppercase Bookshop in Snohomish call themselves Word Nerds. They sell new, second-hand and antiquarian books on two floors of beautifully curated space with old typewriters sitting on some of the shelves. 'I find there is something supernatural that happens when a customer comes to the shop looking for a book,' says Leah. 'If we don't have it, often the title they were looking for turns up in our new stock within days. My favourite strange moment with a customer, though, was when a kid of not more than ten or eleven stopped by, came up to me at the till and whispered, "Where are all the whores?"

'I coughed and spluttered, and asked him to repeat himself.

'He looked at me, exasperated: "You know, the *whooooores*, like Stephen King and Dean Koontz."

'I was so relieved: "Oh, you mean the horr-ors!" And he nodded, claiming that's what he'd said in the first place (it wasn't) – so, thank goodness for that!'

◆

Parnassus Books, Tennessee

In Greek mythology, Mount Parnassus was the home of literature, learning and music. In Nashville, it's the name of a bookshop that's home to the same things. Karen Hayes was a sales rep for Random House when she decided she wanted to open her own bookshop. She didn't have the capital to start the business on her own and was considering setting up a bookstore co-op, when a mutual friend put her in touch with best-selling author Ann Patchett. Ann loved the idea of opening a bookshop: she had the money to support it, but not the time to run it. Karen had the time, but not the money. It was a perfect match.

'Having a mutual friend to introduce us made us both feel more comfortable,' says Karen, 'because initially we didn't know each other at all. It's a big thing setting up a business with someone you don't know. We just had to trust each other. I took an offer of early retirement at Random House, and we started looking for property. Our ideas for the store were different at first, but it soon came together. The timing was perfect in so many ways, but the fact that Ann had a new book coming out was just wonderful. She was interviewed on Diane Rehm and mentioned the bookstore. That was the first time she'd mentioned it in public, and it was at a time when we hadn't found a location, or really settled on a name. It all started to seem very real then, and it just sort of snowballed.

'When we opened on 16 November 2011 we weren't really ready. But the *New York Times* had come down to do a piece on the store the previous week, and it turned out that they were running it that day. I picked up a copy of the newspaper that morning and looked in the arts section and the business section, and there was nothing there, so I just assumed they'd decided not to run it, which was a shame. But then our events manager texted me: "We're on the front page!", and I did a double-take and grabbed the newspaper to take a second look. And there we were – I hadn't even thought to look there! So we had to open that day; if the *New York Times* says you're open, then you're *open*.'

Three thousand people came through the doors of Parnassus on their first day, with mid-morning puppet shows and late-night cheese and wine. Ann says in her essay 'The Bookshop Strikes Back' that she feels as though Karen is a bit of a novelist herself, in the way she's brought her bookshop dream to life. They now have five bookshop dogs, including a beagle called Eleanor Roosevelt Philpott. In the future, Karen hopes to open up a real-life Parnassus on Wheels – a bookmobile that could go from nursing homes to schools, doing book events and partnering up with food trucks and other businesses.

• A CHAT WITH TRACY CHEVALIER •

Tracy Chevalier was born in Washington DC, and now lives in England. She has written seven novels, the latest being *The Last Runaway*, published in 2013. Her second novel, *Girl with a Pearl Earring*, won the Barnes and Noble Discover Award, sold four million copies worldwide, and was made into a film starring Colin Firth and Scarlett Johansson.

" The funny thing about bookshops is that, when I was a kid, we didn't have them in my part of the States. I got my books from the library. It was very much being part of an American community, to go to the library, and I used to go every week. There was a local children's librarian who knew me very well, and she'd always put a book aside for me. The next time I went in, she'd press the book into my hands and say, 'I think you're ready for this.'

I actually got back in touch with my librarian when I was older. I was editing reference books for libraries about writers, and I wrote to her to tell her that I could never have done the editing work I was doing without all the knowledge she gave me by teaching me and getting me to read all those books. I thanked her, and told her that I was thinking about doing an MA in creative writing, to try and become a writer myself. She had Alzheimer's then, but she was at a point where she still understood what I meant. After that, she stopped understanding, but I'm grateful that at least I was able to get that message to her and thank her.

The first connection I actually had with a bookshop was a Waterstones. I did a semester in London in my junior year as an English major; our teacher was an American Professor and there were eighteen of us who came over to England for four months to see theatre and read books. We were meeting near South Kensington and our professor said, 'Now, just around the corner, a new bookshop has opened. It's called Waterstones. It's different from other bookshops: this one has big glass windows, and books out on tables' – which was very unusual back then. I spent a lot of time there.

Since becoming a writer, I've been to a lot of bookshops on tour in the States. I think that it's the big chains that are struggling now, more than the independents. With the big chains, there's been a shift. They used to be these huge places filled with books: now, a lot of the time they are big places just filled with merchandise like games and chocolate. That's a real shame to watch.

I think independents will survive the online threat, and that's because they offer a service in a way that big chains don't. It's not all about price; it's about quality. If big chains want to survive, they're going to have to change the way they're doing things. They need to stop imitating Amazon and do what they do best: be a bookshop, because we need more books and good bookshops.

We're becoming less tangible as people, really: so many things are virtual. I have an e-reader, and I use it sometimes, but when I use it I feel as though everything is floating. I don't associate it with time and place in the same way I do a physical book. At home I've got shelves and shelves of books, and they're real. I've been reading *The Luminaries* for the past two months. That huge bloody book, that's definitely real. It's a good work-out for my arms. I feel physical imprints are happening less and less in the world. Our books and our music are becoming lists on our screens, and we don't have the experience of going somewhere and picking up a book, touching it and taking it home. It's aesthetically unpleasing. Our lives are becoming more convenient but less tangible, and bookshops are the victims of that choice.

Bookshops can also fall victim to themselves; I have seen lazy bookshops. Bookshops that sit back and wait for trade to come to them. When you walk into a bookshop that's putting itself out there, though, that's making an effort – those bookshops make you sit up and listen. Mr. B's, and Topping & Company in Bath [see page 53], Watermark Books at King's Cross [see page 85]: they are excellent. The London Review Bookshop is also excellent – such a non-lazy place. Daunt Books and Foyles are templates of 'How to be a good bookshop.'

A bookshop I love in the States is called Alabama Booksmith, run by Jake Reiss [see page 212], and it's the only bookstore I've been to where all of the books are displayed face-out, so you can display fewer, a lot fewer, but you can see them all properly. It's an amazing experience; all of that work on the cover art: you see it. The owner also has a great connection with local book groups: he knows all of the monthly books for local book groups in case they come in and forget what it is they're supposed to be buying.

The best book event I ever did was with part of the book tour for *Girl with A Pearl Earring*. The book was out in paperback at that point, and no-one really knew who I was – but the best event was at a bookshop in Milwaukee called Harry W. Schwartz (which is now sadly out of business). The bookseller, Nancy, was so wonderful and friendly, and they'd managed to cram 300 people into the store. They'd really made an effort, and there was an incredible buzz in the air. Two days later I was in a chain bookstore in LA, where six people turned up, and my voice was competing with the sound of the coffee machine. So I have a huge fondness for independent bookshops. Tattered Cover in Denver and Powell's in Portland, Oregon are also favourites. Book Passages in California is also wonderful; they do fantastic author events and, after each one, they give the author a box full of personalised stationery. I think it's a lovely touch.

I have to say that the template for the best bookshop in the world, though, is Shakespeare and Company in Paris [see page 112]. I was there a couple of weekends ago with a friend. I took her to the shop, and she was just amazed. There's something about the feel of that place. They do the combination of used and new books so well. It's got a feeling of history in it, and well-chosen books. I love the room in the front upstairs where you're allowed to sit and read as long as you don't take the books out of the room. They still have a bed where authors can stay, and when I first went over to the bookshop in 1982 I hung around hoping that the owner, George, would notice me and hand me a broom crying: 'Sweep the shop, tidy the shelves, read a book, and you can stay!' It didn't happen, sadly, but it did happen to someone else on my course who stayed and had a great time. There's also a wall in the back room upstairs with notes from people who have visited saying how much they loved the place. The notes are all in different languages, and there's a real sense of community there. It's a place where you go and you can really feel as though you're part of something that's bigger than yourself. You should always leave a bookshop like that: feeling inspired and happy. Someone once told me that going into a bookshop made her feel intimidated – like someone going into a wine shop not knowing what they should buy, just seeing a wall of bottles and a snooty owner. A bookshop should never make a customer feel like that, and the good ones never do.

If I worked in a bookshop, something I'd love to hand sell would be *The White Bone* by Barbara Gowdy. It came out fifteen years ago, and it's pretty much off the radar now. I've never read a book with such a convincing, and different, point of view. It's told from the point of view of elephants and you don't feel strange reading it; I was just blown away. I love recommending books. Two friends of mine, Susan Elderkin and Ella Berthoud, are actually bibliotherapists. People go to them with their problems and they recommend books they should read to help them – in the short term, and the long term. They have released a book called *The Novel Cure* which is all about this. If you have a broken heart; if you've been in a car accident; if you have a bad back –

there are recommendations for everything. It's very clever and funny. They did a lot of festivals when the book came out, doing their events in an old ambulance, dressed as nurses, offering therapy sessions.

If I could open a bookshop of my own, I'd stock it by subject to make things more interesting. Books about dreams – non-fiction and fiction – books about quilts, books on countries, so it would be a great place to stumble across something on a subject you're interested in but in the form of a book you had no idea existed. It would be a little messy like that, I suppose, but hopefully brilliant. I think we'd have to have some kind of chocolate in there, too. Perhaps a customer loyalty card system with chocolate rewards – or chocolates hidden around the shop. That would be fun. I'd open the bookshop in a train station, and I'd make it so that people would want to get to the station an hour before their train, just so they could browse. It would have a lot of places to sit, like a waiting room, yet completely filled with bookshelves (and chocolate!), and that exciting possibility of stumbling across the perfect book.

❖

BOOKISH FACT

Walter Swan was born in 1916 and grew up in an old mining town in Arizona. When he was young he enjoyed sharing stories and going on adventures with his big brother, Henry. Later on in life, Walter's wife Deloris said he should start writing some of these stories down, so he did. Walter would recite them, and Deloris would record them, because Walter wasn't very good at spelling. After typing each one up, she'd put it in a box. Within several years the box was overflowing, and Walter decided to send the stories off to publishing companies all across the States. He got rejections from every single one.

In 1990, therefore, when Walter was seventy-four, he took out a loan so that he could pay a Tucson vanity publisher $650 to print 100 hardback copies of his book, *Me 'n' Henry*. Not really knowing much about the bookselling industry, Walter then went around local bookshops to see if they would stock it, and was horrified to discover they would want 40% of the profits if they sold any.

So, what did Walter do? Let them take the profits?

Nope.

Give up?

Nope.

Walter's plan was to open his own bookshop. Not just any bookshop, but one called the One-Book Bookstore: a bookshop that only sold copies of his book, and nothing else. Walter and Deloris remortgaged their house, and opened their shop on Main Street in Bisbee.

How many copies did they manage to sell? Seven thousand!

Walter published three more books, and opened a bookshop next door called the Other Bookstore, so he could sell those there. He said he couldn't possibly sell them in the One-Book Bookstore, because that was just for his first book.

By the time he passed away in 2004 Walter had sold more than 20,000 books.

✶ ✶ ✶ SOME WONDERFUL THINGS ✶ ✶ ✶

◆ The Bookstore Bar in Seattle is indeed a bookstore – in a bar. It has bookshelves up to the ceiling and sells Bookstore Bronco cocktails (sesame-ginger vodka, ginger beer and lime). Book & Bar in New Hampshire also mixes books and booze, and was created by three long-time booksellers and a chef. You can find it inside Portsmouth's old Custom House and Post Office, a building dating back to 1860.

◆ Van Alen Books in New York is an architecture and design bookshop at the Van Alen Institute headquarters in Manhattan. In 2013 they held a competition for architects to re-imagine their bookshop space. The winner was Collective-Lok, and the bookshop is currently being rebuilt under the new design, which is called 'Screen Play.' It involves the use of many different materials to build sliding panels and masks between different sections of the shop, to create an air of mystery. The ceiling will even be used as a display space.

◆ The Elliott Bay Book Company in Seattle has been in business for over forty years, during which time this huge store, with 150,000 titles on beautiful cedar-wood shelves, has hosted over 3,000 author reading events.

◆ OHWOW Book Club is a contemporary art gallery and publisher with retail spaces in both New York and Los Angeles. The bookshop looks like an art installation itself, with shelves like picture frames, in all different shapes and colours, to present the gallery's publications as proper works of art.

- McNally Jackson in New York has a Self-Publishing Department as well as the main bookshop. The company prints self-published books for customers with their Espresso Book Machine, but also offers authors a variety of extra options – to pay for editorial consultations, be put in touch with editors and designers, or have their books displayed out in the bookshop. It's one of the very few bookshops I've seen doing things like this, but I imagine lots more will do so in the future.

- In 2008 Coney Island was home to a bookstore that was also a barber's shop.

- Singularity and Co. in Brooklyn is a science-fiction bookshop. The staff call themselves 'time-travelling archivists': each month they get their customers and their website subscribers to vote for a vintage out-of-print sci-fi book, which Singularity then brings back into print.

- The Heirloom Collection in Charleston, South Carolina, specialises in rare and antiquarian cookbooks. It's located in the French Quarter, home to thirty art galleries all within walking distance of each other along cobbled streets lit with gaslights.

- The Montague Book Mill in Massachusetts jokingly claims to sell 'books you don't need in a place you can't find.' It's a second-hand bookshop inside an 1842 gristmill on the banks of the Sawmill river. It's also got a café, a vinyl store, and is part of an artists' collective.

• A CHAT WITH BILL BRYSON •

Bill Bryson OBE is a best-selling American author of humorous books on travel – such as *Notes from a Small Island* – the English language and science. His acclaimed work of popular science, *A Short History of Nearly Everything*, won the Aventis Prize and the Descartes Prize, and was the biggest-selling non-fiction book of the decade in the UK.

 In Des Moines in Iowa, where I grew up, there was a place called the Bookstore, which mostly sold hardbacks, and then there was a much more popular place called Readers' World, which just sold paperbacks. That's where I used to hang out; it was by the university, and we'd spend hours at a time there. Actually, though – and it seems hardly possible – the heroic company at the time was Borders. In the seventies Borders came into play, and they opened these amazing, huge bookstores in places that wouldn't have had a bookshop otherwise. It seems odd to look back on that now.

As a child, I was handed down a lot of books from my older brother, and I grew up in a family of readers. My parents were both journalists, and my dad had what seemed to me as a little boy an enormous collection of books. In reality it was two bookcases in our living room. I remember from the age of thirteen I started reading those books avidly. I'd take a book down at random, so I discovered everything from Wodehouse to Captain Hornblower novels. I realised that there was something tremendously exciting when it came to reading, and I still believe that, in terms of entertainment, if you find a good book then nothing can match it.

When it comes to bookshops these days, I really like Powell's in Portland, especially their mixture of new and second-hand; I always like it when bookshops put those together. Atmosphere is huge when it comes to a good bookshop. You know you've found a special place when you walk through the door and you just feel comfortable, surrounded by like-minded souls. I also like vastness. A week or so ago I was in a bookshop that I'd forgotten how much I loved, and that's Blackwell's in Oxford. When you go in, it just feels right, and it goes on forever.

One of my favourite bookshops of all time was Central Books on Gray's Inn Road in London. It was on my way to work when I worked at *The Times*, and it was a socialist bookshop specialising in left-wing books. A lot of it was very political, and so much of the shop consisted of obscure titles that you wouldn't find anywhere else. Things on nuclear warheads and prisoners of war. The whole place was a full of a sense of glorious discovery.

Discovery is such an important part of the book industry. There's a book that I just love called *The Ascent of Rum Doodle*, which I came across by accident years ago. I actually helped persuade the publisher to re-issue it and I wrote an introduction to it, too. Good bookshops are full of gems like that: books that are forgotten classics, or books that didn't get the chance to be classics because they weren't discovered properly. In a fantasy world, if I opened a bookshop it would be full of books that you didn't know existed but would be very happy to discover.

One of the things that really impressed me about Britain when I first came here was that you could go to small market towns and, even if there wouldn't be much else there in terms of shops, more often than not there would be a bookshop. Now that's less likely to be the case – though one of my favourite bookshops, Much Ado in Alfriston, is still going. So whilst I don't think I'd ever be brave enough to open up my own bookshop, if I could manipulate the tax system so that there would be more big-hearted bookshops in small places, I would. **„**

✴ ✴ ✴ SOME WONDERFUL THINGS ✴ ✴ ✴

◆ Seminary Co-op Bookstores was set up in Chicago in 1961 by seventeen book-lovers who invested $10 each in the business. Now, more than fifty years later, their collection of academic books in their flagship store on Woodlawn Avenue is considered one of the best in the world.

◆ The Lake Forest Book Store in Illinois was started in 1949 by a group of local women who wanted to provide books for their local community, and over the years it's grown from 650 square feet to 1800 square feet. In the summer author events are held outside in the town square.

◆ Richard Savoy was just twenty-five when he opened Green Apple Books in San Francisco in 1967. He'd been in the army, and also worked as a radio technician, but he loved books more. Green Apple Books is still going strong, and is ten times its original size.

◆ When Adobe Books in San Francisco faced a $4,000-a-month hike in rent in 2013, staff and friends weren't going to stand by and let the place close down. With the permission of the owner they set up an online campaign and raised enough money to turn the bookshop into the membership-based Adobe Books and Arts Co-operative, moved it to a new space, and carried on selling books.

◆ Bart's Books in Ojai, California, has been dubbed the best outdoor bookstore in the world, and I can't say I'm surprised. It has a million titles on bookshelves out in the sunshine, with a 400-year-old oak tree in the middle of it all.

◆ Jenn Witte, who works at Skylight Books in Los Angeles, draws quirky book cover designs, and their bookshop cat Franny has an Instagram account showing things she stared at that day. This amuses me more than it probably should.

◆ Dark Delicacies in Burbank, CA, is America's only all-horror bookshop. Del and Sue Howison started selling horror books on card tables at conventions, and now have their own shop where they sell everything from books on Edgar Allen Poe to hundred-year-old chairs with gargoyles carved into them.

◆ As well as selling new books, the Book Nook in Texas also has a second-hand section where you can fill a bag with books for just $13. For every bagful it sells, the bookshop donates a box of books to troops serving overseas.

• A CHAT WITH BRITTANY CAVALLARO •

Brittany Cavallaro's first collection of poems, *Girl-King*, will be published by the University of Akron Press in 2015. Her poems have appeared in *AGNI*, *Tin House* and the *Best New Poets* anthology. She lives and writes in Milwaukee, Wisconsin.

" So this past fall, something happened between me and Boswell Books, this insanely great indie bookstore here in Milwaukee. Like, I knew it existed before, and I'd bought things there, been to readings, wandered around with a coffee in hand touching things mournfully in the melodramatic way I do when I don't have any money. Except that last part kind of faded away.

I think it started when I realized they stocked the beautiful new editions of Dorothy L. Sayers' Lord Peter Wimsey and Harriet Vane mysteries, and so I bought one… then all the ones they had in stock… and then ordered in the rest. Like you do. It was like eating dessert all the time, except in bed, under a ton of blankets, and it was a Golden Age Mystery dessert, which comes with monocles.

After that, I was just in there every day with a coffee – there's a coffee shop next door – and at least once a week I'd cave and bring something new home. A sparkling-new 'used' copy of Rachel Kushner's *The Flamethrowers*, and Heidi Julavits's *The Vanishers*, as recommended to me by a friend – I can't remember who – because, that's right, when my friends come and visit I bring them to Boswell and spread my hands and feel very self-satisfied, like I've somehow curated this fabulous experience for them. **"**

◆

Singing Wind Bookstore, Benson, Arizona

Winifred Bundy has been selling books at her Singing Wind Bookstore for forty years, and she calls it the 'Headquarters for Books about the South-West.' Singing Wind is a little tricky to find, situated on a working cattle farm four miles from the nearest town. It doesn't have a website, Twitter, Facebook, or email address. It doesn't even have opening hours: you just have to turn up and hope for the best. Yet customers still find it. The bookshelves are all handmade, and Winn bought the bookshop's initial stock with $500 given to her by two astronomers, whose two dogs she'd looked after for a year. If you ask for a title, Winn knows exactly where it is, and has stories to tell you about every single one.

◆

Baldwin's Book Barn, West Chester, Pennsylvania

At this converted 1820s dairy barn filled up with books, a note on a low-hanging beam proclaims: 'Duck or bump!' William and Lilla Baldwin set up their used bookstore in Wilmington in 1934, and moved to the barn in 1946, turning its old milking house into their home. It's now run by their son Tom. The Book Barn is a five-storey building surrounded by six acres of land, with 300,000 old and rare books on 200 subjects, and maps too. There are picnic tables outside where customers can read and relax. The Baldwin family are also descendants of one of the signatories of the Declaration of Independence!

◆

Blue Willow Bookstore, Houston, Texas

A hundred people tweeted or emailed me when Blue Willow Bookstore uploaded a photo of one of their book displays on Twitter: a sign saying

'I can't remember the title, but the book was blue,' surrounded by all the blue books they had in stock. It made me giggle.

'In the past seventeen years, I've seen kids grow up, families move on and new families come in,' says Valerie Koehler, the owner, known as 'Girlboss'.

'We are located in the Energy Corridor with many international energy companies nearby. On any given day, we might hear more than ten languages spoken in the shop. People who love bookstores around the world feel comfortable here. We remind them of home. We're like a neighborhood tavern except we can't sell liquor. Nothing prohibits us from serving it, though!

'Bookselling is always full of strange and wonderful coincidences, whether we're at the bookshop or not. Last week my husband and I were in Costa Rica, 2,500 miles away from our bookshop, and we were eating at a small restaurant when three of my customers walked in!

'I'd love to continue to run the bookshop for a long time, but I suppose all good things must come to an end. My husband wants to retire within five years, which means that I probably won't be far behind him. He wants some land to garden and a place for his winemaking and woodworking. I just want a porch with a view, lots of good books, and a glass or two of wine.'

◆

City Lights, San Francisco

City Lights was America's first all-paperback bookshop, and the first business to be named a literary landmark. It was founded in 1953 by poet Lawrence Ferlinghetti and Peter D. Martin, and became such a literary hotspot that tour buses would pull up outside it, looking for Beat poets. The bookshop is also a publisher, with 200 titles in print: Ferlinghetti was actually arrested for publishing Allen Ginsberg's *Howl and Other Poems,* on the grounds of obscenity. For over fifty years City Lights has fought to promote freedom of speech, and celebrate progressive thinking, principles enshrined in its City Lights Foundation, a non-profit organisation to advance literacy.

◆

Strand Bookstore, New York

Strand Bookstore is the last of the bookshops on what was once called 'Book Row,' but it's an impressive one to still be standing. Book Row once covered six city blocks on Fourth Avenue and contained forty-eight bookshops; Strand opened there in 1927, as a small bookstore run by Ben Bass. Now it's on Broadway and Twelfth Street, houses eighteen miles of books and has 240 employees, as well as a huge warehouse in Brooklyn with another quarter of a million books. The store has been passed down to Ben's son Fred, who now runs it with his daughter Nancy. In December 2013, they had two marriage proposals in the shop, and their best sales day in 86 years! They proudly tweeted the news, signing off, 'Bookstores Are Not Dead!'

◆

The Rebound Bookstore, San Rafael, California

Tim and Joni at the Rebound Bookstore in California have some lovely customer moments to share. They once had a couple stop by on their way to the hospital as the woman was actually in labour, to buy a baby name book.

'We had a large street fair on the road in front of our store once,' says Tim. 'The place was packed with new customers: kids, dogs, teenagers, old folks, everybody. I looked over at a middle-aged guy standing near the history shelves holding a book to his chest. He was crying. I approached him cautiously and asked him if I could do anything to help, and was he OK? He said happily: "Oh, I'm fine. I just want to buy this book." So I told him, sure, and he goes on: "My uncle was killed in the Korean War, but the government would not tell us where he died or how. Maybe they didn't know. But in this book they mention his unit, his squadron, and his name, along with the story of how he was killed. This is closure for my family after almost seventy years." He smiled: "How much is the book?" I smiled back, and gave him a discount.

'On our street in San Rafael, California, there's a training facility for the world-famous Guide Dogs for the Blind. There are blind people up and down the street all the time learning to deal with their dogs. One sunny summer afternoon my wife was in the store by herself and half a dozen blind people came in the store, accompanied by a mentor. They told her that they had readers who read stories to them, and they wanted her to recommend some of her favourite books to buy. That's when I pulled up outside the front of the store, and could see Joni through the window. She was telling stories and reading dust jackets, gesturing the characters, doing the voices, etc. – everything from Dumas to Garrison Keillor, *Schindler's List*, Ken Kesey, Amy Tan, Ken Follett… They bought about a dozen books and were very happy about it.

'Another local phenomenon in Marin County, California, is that the place is noted for its cultural focus on alternative philosophies. There are numerous large and small meditation centres and retreat locales where the focus is on meditation, inner development and "mindfulness"… up to a point. One afternoon my wife, sitting in her office, heard a most un-mindful sound: a voice shouting, "I wanted that book!" She came out to see two men literally fighting over a cook book. One man had taken the book off the shelf just before the other man had reached for it. He was the one doing the screaming. The other man rolled his eyes and relinquished the book. The man who went over the top – and got his book – came up to the counter to buy it. It turned out that it was the chef at a local Zen meditation centre! Ommm, indeed!'

❖

BOOKISH FACT

For the last few years of his life, Ernest
Hemingway was sure he was being
followed. He was actually given electric
shock treatment fifteen times because of
this, as doctors thought that he was
paranoid and hallucinating.

It emerged many years later that
Hemingway had not been hallucinating
at all. In fact he had been put under
surveillance by the head of the FBI because
he used to be a KGB spy. Hemingway had
been recruited by the Soviets in 1941, and
even made a trip to China where he was
given the cover name 'Argo'. The KGB
eventually gave up on him because he
wasn't very good at his job.

• A CHAT WITH KRISTEN KAUFFMAN •

THE STORY OF THE PEREGRINE BOOK COMPANY

" Our fast-paced world wants to tempt readers out of the bookstores onto their e-readers, but there are still some communities that prefer a bookstore. In my small town in Arizona we relied on a chain bookstore until the mall tripled the rent, and the corporate office decided to close the branch instead of negotiating costs. While the bookstore had been my whole world – I worked there – it became obvious over its last two months that it had also been some customers' whole world, too. We had book-lovers, students, and retirees writing letters to the company head office, writing letters to the bookstore itself, and staging protests outside our doors to make a statement: *We want our bookstore.*

It's hard to lament the loss of such a huge chain bookstore when they have been, in part, responsible for putting indies out of business, but something interesting happened here. A local businessman realised the void that would grow in our town and decided to start an indie bookstore of his own. Then came a collaboration. A few writing teachers at the community college banded with this businessman, with one of the booksellers at the chain bookstore, and a retired librarian from another local college.

We asked questions like, 'What do people look for in a bookstore? What do people need in a bookstore?' We all agreed that freedom of speech and freedom of expression should be the foundations, but community was important, too. The business owner decided to embrace community through events like open mic poetry readings and author signings; through hosting events to bring writers together with comic book lovers and local artists.

But then something else happened. The old chain bookstore, once an enemy of indies around the country, decided to help kick-start our new indie bookstore. Patrons of the company offered to donate trailers full of books to help us get started. The manager of the closed branch generously donated every single available bookshelf, display, table, and fixture. Local antique stores gave comfy wing-backed chairs. The message was clear from the people of our town: we want a bookstore, and we're going to do everything we can to pitch in.

Now when you walk into the Peregrine Book Company in Prescott, Arizona, you can see this fantastic presence of community. Antiques blend with chain bookstore features for a store that holds used and new books. There is a mural of a forest in the children's department painted by a local artist. The bookshelf next to one of the registers features local art, and then there's 5,000 square feet of books, as well as a stage for authors to read aloud to customers.

This is more than an indie bookstore built with many hands. This is home. **"**

Kristen Kauffman is a novelist, freelance writer and creative writing teacher. She values her ~~support group~~ book club, and maintains that there may be enough time in our lives to read all of the books we buy. Just maybe.

✱ ✱ ✱ SOME WONDERFUL THINGS ✱ ✱ ✱

◆ John K. King Used & Rare Books in Detroit has twenty employees, two dogs and two canaries. The bookshop is inside a huge glove factory from the 1940s.

◆ The Spotty Dog, Beer & Ale near the Hudson River in New York is inside a 1800s fire station. It sells thousands of books as well as serving hand-crafted ale from local brewers, with rows of bar stools where the fire engines used to line up.

◆ Happy Tales Bookshop in Markesan, Wisconsin has a million books in six different buildings around a farm. Some of the stock is kept in a huge converted manure tank that's been re-designed to look like a castle.

◆ The Brattle Book Shop in Boston, founded in 1825 and run by the Gloss family since 1949, is one of the oldest bookshops in America. There are three floors of books to browse, and in sunny weather there are bookstalls outside. It once sold a signed photograph of Abraham Lincoln for $75,000.

◆ Politics and Prose in Washington DC is famous for its author events, some of which are broadcast on cable. Recently it set out to resurrect the idea of the 'Literary Lunch' at the nearby Willard Hotel – 150 years old and rather beautiful – mixing elegant food with bookish events.

- The Book Barn in Connecticut is definitely an experience bookshop, with everything from books to a petting zoo. The books are housed in various shacks and buildings, with names like the Annex, Hades, the Haunted Bookshop and the Last Page.

- Square Books in Oxford, Mississippi, is actually three bookshops about 100 feet apart, called Square Books, Off Square Books and Square Books Jr. They specialise in Southern literature, and even have their own radio station.

- Village Books in Bellingham, Washington run the *Chuckanut Radio Hour*, which includes skits with authors and customers, and many different book clubs – the Environmental Conservation Book Group, for example, discussing contemporary and classic writings on environmental issues.

- The Last Bookstore in Los Angeles is a 15,000-square-foot bookshop, record store and café. One section, the Labyrinth, has a tunnel made out of books, and all the titles there are $1. The building used to be a bank, and the underground vaults have been turned into reading rooms.

• A CHAT WITH KAT ZHANG •

Author of the *Hybrid Chronicles*: *What's Left of Me* and its sequels.

"When I was younger I didn't visit bookstores nearly as much as libraries. But I've been lucky to have some wonderful indie bookstores near me these past few years. Back in Nashville, where I used to live, there was Parnassus. I did some of my first book events there, and I just love the atmosphere – everything from the stars hanging down from the ceiling to the genres written on chalkboards over the tall shelves. Here in Atlanta, where I now live, I'm particularly partial to the Little Shop of Stories. It's really amazing how much they do for the community, not only as a place to buy books, but also as a place for local kids to have summer camps and reading groups and meet their favorite authors."

◆

The Alabama Booksmith, Birmingham

Jake Reiss's Alabama Booksmith is pretty unique in that it only stocks signed copies. All the books are face out on the shelves, too, so you can see them properly.

As of 1990, Jake was the only male member of his family for two generations not to be a bookseller – so he decided to change that.

'The fact that my oldest son and younger brother were both booksellers had no effect,' he jokes. 'However, when my youngest son opened a used bookstore, after managing a large operation in San Francisco, this appeared a great way to make lots of money and meet girls. That did influence me to open our shop.'

In 1999 they moved to a new location. 'At first sight family, friends and customers saw a dilapidated, deserted office building hidden from sight by wild trees, vines and weeds,' says Jake. 'We saw a cosy bookstore with a fireplace, ice-cold water fountain, custom-made shelves and counters, immaculate rest rooms, office and storage space to squander, and 125 parking spaces.

'We bought that ugly duckling, and after bulldozing, replacing the floor and ceilings, hiring a master woodcraftsman, replacing the plumbing and doubling the existing square footage with a new building for office and storage, the beautiful swan was ready to spread its wings in ninety days. Then there was this minor problem of transporting 100,000 books. Forty customers volunteered, and the all-new and improved Alabama Booksmith opened as our dream store.

'The bookshop has taken over my life. I've become a very boring person who works ten to twelve hours a day, and then goes home and reads. Only a small percentage of all readers have any interest in the upper-level literary fiction and non-fiction titles we select, and fewer still really care if a copy is hardback or paperback, first edition or later printing, and signed or un-signed. However, that tiny little group we target is tenacious and, as far as we know, we're the only bookstore on the planet that carries exclusively signed copies at regular price. The result is that we have customers in all fifty states and dozens of international purchasers.'

◆

Book People, Austin, Texas

I am forever impressed by Book People in Austin, which is the largest bookshop in the state of Texas, and for the past fifteen years has been voted best bookstore in town. The owner, Steve Bercu, has customers that love the bookshop so much it's able to sell its own merchandise (pens, T-shirts, mugs… you name it; they have it).

There is a massage chair in the middle of the shop; the cookery section is peppered with fridges and other kitchen utensils; the teenage section is carefully separate from the children's section (Steve jokes that it's painted black to heighten feelings of angst); and they hold birthday par-ties in the bookshop two or three times a week. They host 400 author events a year, and 200 story times for children, all in the shop's small theatre. They also run book festivals not only in Texas but nearly 2000 miles away in Boston and Philadelphia, as well as themed literary summer camps (such as one for Harry Potter fans). Last summer children from eleven different countries signed up to go.

Words Across the World is a community-wide project the bookshop runs in conjunction with Random House and the Austin Independent School District, using reading to educate the children of Austin about other parts of the world, and also raising money and donating books to those who don't have access to them. So far children from over forty local schools have been encouraged to read about Malawi in Shana Burg's *Laugh with the Moon*, and in turn paired up with school children in Africa as part of the bookshop's international pen pal programme. The store's customers can also buy books from its 'Giving Tree' to be sent to Africa along with the books Random House gives to schools in Malawi, or donate money to the charity World Altering Medicine to go towards medical supplies.

◆

WORKS, Searsport, Maine

Karen Jelenfy first tried her hand at bookselling in her aunt's bookshop, Old Monterey Books in California. Later, when she moved to Searsport, a small village that didn't have a bookshop, she decided she had to open one.

'I knew that every town worth its salt should have a bookstore,' she says. 'WORKS is a curated collection of books put together by me with the assistance of my "pickers" – folks with different tastes and areas of expertise to mine. This makes for a very diverse selection of books, most of which are used and a few of which are new. My pickers and I are artists, and writers, and boat builders, and waitresses and... WORKS feels as much like a library as it does a store – a library where you get to keep your choices!

'The bookshop also includes my other two passions: art and craft. There is an art gallery in the back of the shop, and a knitting and spinning supply area in the front. I also had a Sock Crank in once, when people could try an early industrial hand-cranked sock machine.

'I have many great customers: there's Bob the Elder, local plant expert; Bob the Younger, famous painter; Charlie, who collects Edward Corey; Sister Bette, who is a weaver, and comes to buy wool; Angie, who loves anything about Paris... Having someone come in, choose a book, and sit in a chair is still my favourite customer moment.'

◆

Wild Rumpus, Minneapolis

Wild Rumpus is filled with books... and animals. Tilly and Pip are two little rats who live under the floorboards in a glass cage, so you can watch them running around. There are also two chinchillas, Amelia and Mr Skeeter; two ferrets, Doodle and Ferdinand; three cats, two doves, three cockatiels, two chickens, a lizard called Spike and a tarantula who goes by the name of Thomas Jefferson. Oh, and the bookshop door has a purple child-size door built into it, so children can let themselves in.

• A CHAT WITH HANK GREEN •

Hank Green is an American entrepreneur, musician and vlogger, based in Missoula, Montana. He's well-known for his YouTube channel Vlog-Brothers, where he regularly uploads videos along with his brother John Green. He's also the founder of Project for Awesome, and VidCon.

> ❝ I fell in love with stories. Books were a way to understand the world, and people, better without leaving my house (or even my head).

We've got some great bookshops here in Missoula. There's one called Shakespeare and Co. Booksellers that's nice and small and has a couple of comfy chairs. And the Book Exchange always has discounts on treasures I couldn't find anywhere else. I tend to like smaller stores because, even when they don't have what I'm looking for, they have something I want, even if I didn't know I wanted it.

I don't think bookshops will change that much in the future. They'll still be beautiful and helpful and cozy and wonderful. It's easy to underestimate physicality in today's world. I mean, the machine I'm typing on has access to more words than any bookshop in the world. But a curated, physical information space is maybe more valuable because of that, not less. We need curation. Access to everything is eventually paralysing.

If I could open up my own bookstore? I'd open a place that's only for people who really love books. All genres would be welcome, but there would be no paperbacks in the whole place – and if you rip a dust cover, you're banned for life... **"**

◆

Community Bookstore, Brooklyn, New York

• A CHAT WITH DAN WILBUR •

Dan Wilbur is a comedian living in Brooklyn, New York. He is the creator of betterbooktitles.com and the author of *How Not to Read*. He used to work at Park Slope's Community Bookstore.

" I once asked the co-owner of Community Bookstore, Stephanie Valdez, what the mission statement of the store was. After a few moments we didn't land on a modus operandi but rather a single image of what Stephanie wanted to see every day: a mother reading a book to her child.

Park Slope is not short on moms nor children. Achieving Stephanie's goal was as simple as opening the doors every day.

Fitting strollers in, however, looks borderline impossible for how cosy the store is. Still, the moms seem to manage. When you enter the Community Bookstore, the first thought is that there couldn't possibly be this many books in this small a space in New York City. New York is all about compartmentalizing. Or trying to, anyway. People are constantly trying to squeeze something into a space that's too small to keep it. They're trying to separate themselves from the noise on the street by sneaking into a quiet haven like a bookstore. But everything in New York bubbles over into spaces it shouldn't. Nothing can be quarantined. The Community Bookstore is in the heart of New Parents-ville, sure. But parents are never just parents.

Trying to squeeze the customer type at Community Bookstore into one small shape is equally impossible. Enter the store at 11 a.m. and walk to the back. You'll find the wished-for mother reading to her child. Wander a few minutes and look at the back-yard where two turtles stand immobile on the rocks of a pond in the store's backyard. After a few minutes of Zen, walk back into the store where you will find the same mom you saw earlier, now up front debating with a member of staff on the merits of a certain famous author – one who could very well be in the store eavesdropping. More likely the mom is talking about her own published works. Or her current life as a tenured professor teaching Comparative Lit at a college. In Brooklyn it's never just a mom reading to her child.

The best way to describe the mixture of vibes the Community Bookstore is stuck between, is to tell you its geographical location: it's nestled between a large toy store on one side and a wine store that's been serving the community for forty-five years on the other. If a quiet place to read new fiction – stuck between booze and baby toys – doesn't epitomize Park Slope, I don't know what does. **99**

❖

BOOKISH FACT

In 2008, Gabriel Levinson started
spending his weekends cycling around
public parks in Chicago on his
custom-built Book Bike. The bike had a
box built around it that folded out to
display 300 titles. Gabriel gave books
away to anyone who promised they
would read them.

• A CHAT WITH AUDREY NIFFENEGGER •

Audrey Niffenegger is a writer and artist living in Chicago. She is the author of, amongst other things, the international bestseller *The Time Traveler's Wife* and *Her Fearful Symmetry*.

❝ I have a lot of different relationships with books. I'm a reader, I'm a writer, and then there are the books I actually make myself. With those, I'm thinking about the outside of the book almost as much as what's inside: I'll be making up the story, drawing pictures, printing and binding. At the end there'll be a dozen books, or a hundred, depending on what I want to create. Those books, I feel, are completely mine because I have made every decision about the way they are. But I enjoy writing things that are going to be put out via commercial channels just as much as the ones I make myself. I think it's healthy, and exciting, to try lots of different things. I do whatever I'd like to do at that particular moment in time. I figure whatever I choose to create, I'll be neglecting somebody – so my art may as well make me happy.

It's an amazing feeling when a publisher sends you your book for the first time, and you can hold it. Encountering the books in the wild, though, is even more surreal. I saw *The Time Traveler's Wife* for the first time in Women & Children First in Chicago, which is one of my favourite places. I'd been going there for decades, so it seemed completely bizarre that one day something of mine should be casually sitting on a table there.

Women & Children First is owned by Linda Bubon and Ann Christophersen, and they've been partners since the beginning. They've recently put the business up for sale, as they're retiring, so it's an end of an era, really, but the bookshop will live on under someone else's watch. It's one of those bookshops where you can immediately detect its goodness. It's a feminist bookshop, and is very much a progressive and socially aware place. They also have amazing children's books and the best story times. People are pretty fierce about supporting local bookshops in Chicago.

In London, I'm a huge fan of the London Review Bookshop, and all the funny little shops on Cecil Court. I love exploring because, even though the same titles might appear on the shelves in London as they do back home in Chicago, they're often different editions, so it's as though I'm stepping into an alternate universe with books I never knew existed.

When you say 'bookshop' you can mean so many different things, especially, I think, in America. The bookshop scene, like the country, changes so much depending on what state you're in. There's Faulkner House Books in New Orleans, which is tiny, and then there's King's in Detroit, which is vast – warehouse sized. They have a section of rare books which they're very nervous about letting you into, but it's incredible, and if your taste doesn't fit the mainstream, then you'll probably find something you'll love.

I'm a big fan of the book as an object, too, and I have a tendency to stuff things inside them: bus transfers, receipts, pictures, even obituaries if the author has died recently. With a physical book you can add stories to the stories they already have. Something I really like is books that are 'extra-illustrated.' In Chicago there's the Newberry Library, and the Wing Collection is their collection on the history of books and printing. They have well over 100,000 books now, but it was started by a man called John M. Wing, who liked to extra-illustrate books. So, in his copy of *Hamlet* he'd put in copies of every painting of Hamlet and his dad's ghost that he could find. So these books became unique, because he was altering them. It's a super-over-active form of reading.

There used to be a wonderful, tiny bookshop chain in Chicago called Kroch's & Brentano. They were the bookshop of my childhood. They were famous for their art book section, which was run by a man called Henry who was rather fierce. I remember being very scared of him when I was thirteen or fourteen. After that, I loved Bookman's Alley. Roger Carlson was the owner, and that shop was incredible because it was in a carriage house. I never really looked at the building properly until he'd sold most of the books (he just recently closed), and I stood back and realised that the building was really quite decrepit. You never noticed it because it was so full – you couldn't see the walls, or most of the floor, due to the books. Roger's great because he collected odd furniture and odd little antiques, so the western section would have a saddle, and the sports section would have peculiar old nick-nacks representing team mascots. You could never see all of the bookshop; it was inexhaustible. Roger is also a fan of the art and history of printing, so his bookshop had a full-size Chandler and Price press, and all these books on typography. I was constantly able to find books on printing that I'd never seen before.

Roger is the kind of bookseller I am sure will exist again in the future; it's just that it takes a long time to make people like him. They grow over time, inhaling the text of the books that they read – I mean, Roger didn't even start his bookshop until he was fifty. I was terribly sad when he closed the shop, but he's getting on in years and his health had started to deteriorate. I loved his shop so much that I've even written about it – twice, actually. Roger is in *The Time Traveler's Wife* as a bookshop owner, and Bookman's Alley features in the series I'm writing at the moment, where two characters travel to bookshops in the process of closing. Their job is to capture the spirit of Bookman's Alley, so that it can live on elsewhere. This series is called 'The Library' (*The Night Bookmobile* being the first in that batch), and the stories are concerned with an eternal library, which is essentially the afterlife.

Over the past few years, I've been thinking about opening my own bookshop. At the moment, Chicago doesn't have a specialist artists' books bookshop, so I'd love to start something that's both an art bookshop and a permanent collection. A kind of museum-library, where I'd stock things from crazy hand-made artists' project books to little Xerox magazines, comics and art books. Things made by artists, and things about artists. I've been looking for a building that will give me the right kind of space, and thinking about how it would work. You see, I've done my share of retail work in the past, and I'm not sure I was ever any good at it. So I'd have to hire someone to work there for me, I think, and I would be behind the scenes. For a long time, I wanted to call the shop 'The Library,' but I think that might be a little too confusing when it comes to people Googling...

While the real estate crisis was going on, I was scouting for buildings hoping to find somewhere, but I've yet to find the perfect place. I looked at some crazy buildings. One was built in 1927, in Lincoln Park, and it was a huge neo-classical bank building, all done up in beautiful white terracotta. Above the main doorway the word 'Perfection' was engraved, and when I saw it I thought, 'Oh my God, I want that building.' But it's huge and the heating bill would be ridiculous. I've also looked at a Christian Science Church in Chicago's Hyde Park, near a cluster of other bookshops. It was built in the 1920s, gorgeous, lots of gold-leaf... but the floors have been covered with moss, and there's mould all over the walls. We had to enter the place wearing hard hats and it felt as though we were walking through a forest. I decided against buying the place, because it would cost way too much to restore, but there was a moment when I was walking through it, and the light was shining through on the green walls and... I don't know. It seemed almost like a holy space. I thought, for a moment, perhaps I could build a conservatory or a greenhouse inside the walls and keep all the books inside that. But then I'm a writer, and I am good at coming up with imaginary bookshops which have no business sense whatsoever...

I've had other ideas for shops in the past, such as a shop that's only open late at night, and is terribly lit, so you'd have to go around groping for things, not really knowing what you were buying. Everything would be black – hats, clothes, vinyl, cats… Perhaps a little silly, but fun to imagine. My perfect bookshop, on the other hand, is a whole different project: it's something I definitely want to bring to life. **"**

Central and South America

❖

BOOKISH FACT

Luis Soriano, a teacher in La Gloria, Colombia, is the founder of the Biblioburro: a travelling library on the back of a donkey. Luis and his two donkeys, Alfa and Beto, travel around the local area, lending books to local children who don't have access to bricks and mortar libraries.

Luis wants to make sure the future generations of La Gloria are given as many opportunities as possible, and believes that literature is the way to make that happen. He has also set up Cine al Campo, showing world cinema and documentaries to the local children.

◆

El Ateneo Grand Splendid, Buenos Aires, Argentina

El Ateneo is widely considered to be one of the most beautiful book-shops in the world. It's situated inside Teatro Grand Splendid, opened in 1919 as a theatre with ceiling frescoes and pillars sculpted as human figures, that in the 1920s hosted tango competitions and radio broad-casts. In 1929, it became a cinema and showed the first talking films in Argentina.

In 2000 the cinema seats were removed, and the building was con-verted into a bookshop. It still retains an old-worldly, dramatic ambi-ence, with its domed, painted ceiling, gold decorations and heavy red curtains framing the proscenium arch, but now bookshelves line the stalls, balconies and galleries, and there's a café on the stage. It's pretty breath-taking, and over a million people visit it every year.

◆

The Livraria da Vila, Sao Paolo, Brazil

On each floor of the Livraria da Vila massive circles are cut out of the ceiling; this is architect Isay Weinfeld's re-invention of the concept of 'open plan', so that customers looking up can see the books arrayed on the floors above. Rotating glass-covered bookcases serve as the book-shop's doors.

◆

El Péndulo, Mexico

El Péndulo (The Pendulum) is a beautiful café-bookshop that has be-come so popular there are now six branches across the country. The Polanca branch has trees growing inside the bookshop itself; at Zona Rosa a bar called 'Bukowski's Bar' honours the Beat poets.

❖

BOOKISH FACT

Raúl Lemesoff is the founder of the Arma de Instrucción Masiva – Weapon of Mass Instruction – which is a Book Tank. Raúl obtained a 1979 Ford Falcon from the Argentine armed forces and modified it to look like a military tank. He then mounted bookshelves on the exterior, and now travels around Buenos Aires in it, handing out books for free.

Raúl set up the Book Tank in protest of government propaganda, claiming that education is the weapon of the masses. He aims to spread peace through literature.

◆

Librería Nosotrx, Santiago, Chile

At Librería Nosotrxs in Chile you are forced to come at things from a different angle. Most of the bookshelves are arranged on a diagonal, so customers have to tilt their heads to read the spines. The stock is also chosen with a desire to present alternative views of the world. The shop was originally established to promote books by and for women, and so fight for freedom through art and culture, and now retains a general agenda of human rights, and a firm belief in what it calls 'bibliodiversity'.

✳ ✳ ✳ SOME WONDERFUL THINGS ✳ ✳ ✳

◆ Livraria Cultura was founded in Brazil by Eva Herz in 1947. There are now nineteen bookshops across the country, including the Sao Paulo branch, the largest bookshop in Brazil, which opened in 2007 inside an old theatre, with a huge dragon sculpture hanging from the ceiling.

◆ The Spitting Llama Bookshop in Copacabana, Bolivia, on the bank of the biggest lake in South America, Lake Titicaca, sells books in thirty different languages, as well as hiking equipment.

◆ Often hailed as the best bookshop in Ecuador, Librería Rayuela – Hopscotch Bookshop – wants to create a space where the smell of new books mixes with the sound of music to create an over-all sense of well-being.

◆ In 2011, Marta Minujin built a twenty-five-metre-high tower of books in San Martin Square in Buenos Aires, from 30,000 titles in all languages, to celebrate the city becoming the World Book Capital that year. She called it the Tower of Babel.

◆ El Mercado de las Brujas – the Witches' Market – in La Paz, Bolivia, is located in a mountain clearing. It's run by local witch doctors, known as *yatiri*, and sells spell books, dried frogs, amulets, powders and medicinal plants. The strangest of all its goods are dried llama foetuses, which Bolivians often bury around their houses as offerings to their earth mother, the goddess Pachamama.

Australasia

❖

BOOKISH FACT

In 2010, to celebrate the thirtieth
birthday of their signature furniture piece,
the Billy bookcase, IKEA lined thirty of
them along Bondi Beach, and filled them
with books, making this the world's longest
outdoor bookcase. Surfers and sunbathers
were able to swap a book from the shelves
with one of their own, or make a donation
to buy one. All money raised went to
the Australian Literacy and Numeracy
Foundation.

◆

Gertrude & Alice Café Bookshop, Bondi Beach

Gertrude & Alice Café Bookshop, named after the celebrated literary couple who ran a famous literary salon in Paris in the early twentieth century, calls itself an oasis for writers, readers, coffee-lovers and thespians. The author Katerina Cosgrove, who opened it with Jane Turner, says she was influenced by the slick art and design-based bookshops in Berlin, the antiquarian booksellers that double as rug-merchants in the Grand Bazaar of Istanbul, and open-air teahouses on the islands and in the mountain villages of Greece. She was also inspired by the faded bohemian grandeur of Shakespeare and Company, 'but even more so,' she says, 'by the stories of Gertrude Stein and Alice B. Toklas, and those by Hemingway and Joyce. I read Hemingway's *A Moveable Feast* in Paris and followed in his footsteps, sitting in the Jardin du Luxembourg among pink roses, drinking cold white wine and eating potatoes with olive oil.'

Jane explains how they created their bookshop:

'I like to think that the influences of Gertrude Stein and Alice B. Toklas somehow found their way into our little Bondi Beach shop, and that they had a lot to say about the design and ambience of the place.

'Katerina and I met at Sappho Books in Glebe, Sydney [see page 237] where I was working part-time. She had returned from a trip to Greece and I loved hearing the stories of her travels and experiences. She had just written her first novel *The Glass Heart,* and when it was published she introduced me to many new writers and books, and our friendship began there. She had always planned to open another bookshop with a café, and in 1999 she asked me to join her. It completely changed my life. Katerina had opened cafés before, so she had a vision of what she wanted. Finances were tight, and there were lots of mishaps in the initial stages, but we did it. It now seems like a long time ago. Unfortunately the many demands of running a busy café-bookstore took their toll on Katerina's writing: she only stayed in the business for nine months and then left to write full-time. I have owned the bookshop myself since 2001.

'It was always our intention to create a space where our customers would feel inspired to do whatever they wanted. We knew that we would attract a lot of writers – it is a wonderful space to write in. Books, films, screenplays, poems and even PhDs have been written in our shop: we've been credited in films and book acknowledgements more times than we can count. Champagne has always been opened when a deal was brokered or a book finished, and shared amongst the customers. We became a bit of a haven for out-of-work actors as well, and we felt it was a little like the Saturday night soirées that were hosted by Gertrude and Alice at 27 Rue de Fleurus, with lots of interesting people sitting around sharing stories and discussing life, eating wholesome food and drinking café au lait!

'Getting the balance right between the café and bookstore has been difficult at times. The demands of the café and its noises, delicious smells and chaos often win over the quiet, organisation and solitude needed of a bookshop. Somehow, though, the combination works, and now I'm afraid to change things too much. People seem to like it just the way it is.

'We have had people walk in and tell us they have been told about our bookshop from friends who were travellers. In fact, it happened today with a couple from England! They said it looked just like their home but without all their clothes thrown everywhere.

'After so many years customers become our friends, and we like it that way. The children to whom we serve their first "babycinos", and who sit on our laps while we read them *Possum Magic* by Mem Fox, eventually go off to school and come in and show us how they can read by themselves.

'We hosted a wedding just a few months after we opened, when Andy Whitfield, the actor who starred in *Spartacus*, and who passed away a few years ago, married his beautiful wife Vashti. We created a Tuscan feast and transformed the bookstore, and it was a special night. We have been visited by many famous people who have really enjoyed the space – Heath Ledger, Claire Danes, Ewan McGregor and Orlando Bloom to name a few. It's always exciting to have a celebrity drop in and buy a book. Russell Crowe called in this summer to buy a copy of Christos Tsiolkas' new book *Barracuda*.

'I will never forget the opportunity that Katerina gave me – but now it's my space and my vision. I used to have her signs and handwriting everywhere to keep a sense of her in the space. I did this mostly because I really missed her – we made a great team together. The bookshop has now become a huge part of my life. It ends up being that way because you are open fifteen to sixteen hours a day, seven days a week, managing twenty-five staff at a time. Knowing that people love and appreciate the bookshop the way I do is a huge motivation for me. It is definitely what keeps me going. My love of books and reading – and our amazing customers.'

◆

Clunes, Victoria

Clunes became Victoria's first ever gold town in the mid-nineteenth century, where gold was mined for fifty years. Now it's Australia's Book Town. It has eight permanent bookshops, the largest being Index On Literature, and in 2007 their first book festival, Book Town for a Day, attracted 6,000 visitors. So many people came that they ran out of everything: food, water, and even electricity! As that was such a success, they now hold a two-day festival every May which 20,000 people attend. Horse-drawn carts bring book-lovers to Clunes from the railway station, sixty book traders set up shop and the children's centre is designed so children feel as though they are walking into a book.

✳ ✳ ✳ SOME WONDERFUL THINGS ✳ ✳ ✳

◆ Barbara Burdon loved to travel. Her husband, Tom, a marine biologist, had travelled all over the world. In the 1960s, she started selling maps in a converted flat under her house in Macquarie, Canberra. In the 1970s, she bought a whole library of books on China, and in the 1980s, with the help of her daughter Sally, Asia Bookroom was born, specialising in books on Asia and the Middle East. Recently it moved to new premises nine times the size of the original shop.

◆ Archives Fine Books in Brisbane is one of the largest second-hand bookshops in the world. You can find it inside a heritage-listed building owned by the Australia Koala Foundation.

◆ Storytime in Whangarei, New Zealand was opened in 1982 by five young mothers who wanted their children, and the children of their local community, to have access to the best books they could find.

◆ The Book Nook in Queensland is Australia's oldest performing arts bookshop. Actors and students go there before auditions; its booksellers are famous for being able to track down the perfect drama text suited to any type of role.

◆ Alias Grace in Woodville is a bookshop and art gallery run by Rosie and her mum Sonja. Sonja also helps re-home retired greyhounds – so you may well spy some at the bookshop.

◆ Electric Shadows Bookshop in Canberra opened in 1987, connected with an art house cinema. Its 'Electric Wall' is devoted to exhibitions of book-related art.

- Gawler Books in Willaston is actually a house built in the 1880s. Five rooms are filled with books.

- The Underground Bookshop in Coober Pedy, South Australia, is indeed an underground bookshop, inside an old opal mine.

- Unity Books in New Zealand says that for over forty-five years it has relied on two kinds of daily traffic: a wonderful mix of people, and a great selection of books. They've expanded over the years and now have a permanent microphone for bookshop gigs, as well as still having a great selection of books (though they admit that they do have 'a lamentable section of vampire porn'.)

- The Little Bookroom in Melbourne opened in 1960 and was the first bookshop in Australia to only sell children's books. Their shop sign is an original ink illustration by Edward Ardizzone.

- Sappho Books is in an 1880s building in Glebe, New South Wales, filled with antiquarian books. Out back, there's a courtyard with a sneaky wine and tapas bar. Upstairs is the DaCapo Music Bookstore, a self-service bookshop.

- 'Florilegium' (flower-gathering), derives from the Greek 'anthologia', meaning a collection of stories, as flowers were often symbols of finer literature. The Florilegium Bookshop in Sydney specialises in books on botany, with texts on everything from moon-planting to Peruvian cacti.

- The Bodhi Tree bookshop in Mount Hawthorn, Perth sells books to enhance physical and mental well-being. There is an in-house writing coach, and it also offers philosophy classes and has an organic juice bar.

- Cook the Books in Auckland, which has the largest selection of cookery books in New Zealand, houses a demonstration kitchen, and runs private cookery classes with its in-house chef.

- Berkelouw Books' Book Barn in Berrima, Wingecarribee is filled with timber beams, cathedral-style vaulted ceilings and a huge stone fireplace. There's also a Bar and Grill, wine tastings, and you can get married in amongst the bookshelves, too.

- During International Free Comic Day in 2010, comic book lovers dressed up as their favourite action heroes. The owner of the Adelaide Comic Centre, Michael Baulderstone, dressed up as Spiderman. That afternoon, he spotted someone trying to steal comics from his shop, so he ran out from behind the counter, and chased after them. Once he'd caught the thief, he shouted for someone to call the police, and asked others to block the door. Since Michael was dressed up as Spiderman, it took his customers a while to realise that this wasn't a publicity stunt; once they cottoned on, a couple of people dressed as Jedi knights jumped up and blocked the exit, to make sure that the shoplifter couldn't get away.

Asia

❖

BOOKISH FACT

Lewis Carroll's *Alice in Wonderland* was banned in China in 1931, as General Ho Chien thought it was offensive to depict animals talking as if they were people.

China

◆

钟书阁: Shanghai

In the Songjiang District, you can find the most beautiful bookshop in Shanghai: a two-storey building with a spire, which has been transformed into the 钟书阁 (Bell Book Club) bookshop by Alex Fang.

The interior was designed using Flying Star Feng Shui, with nine square rooms in the bookshop to represent different areas of thought. There's even a secret mediation room containing a single chair, where customers can shut out the rest of the world. In one room, panelled with dark wood and illuminated by eerie yellow lighting, there are books not only on the shelves but also stretching out in rows under a transparent floor. It creates a strange bookish vertigo: customers find themselves surrounded by books in all directions. The next room, by contrast, could not be more open: a square white floor, white wood with clear glass bookcases, and a mirrored ceiling that reflects bright light everywhere, as though the customers are walking around inside a cloud.

◆

KID'S REPUBLIC, Beijing

KID'S REPUBLIC is a bookshop ergonomically designed for children by SAKO Architects. The bookcases are all different sizes, covered in rainbow-patterned carpet, and slope down to the floor at either end to encourage children to climb up and walk along them. Circular alcoves have been carved out of the middle of each set of shelves and lined with brightly-coloured cushions, for kids to climb inside and read.

◆

Librairie Avant-Garde, Nanjing

There's a road in Nanjing that slopes down a hill and disappears into the ground. It used to be a 4,000 square-metre underground car park, and before that a bomb shelter, but now it's home to one of the most unusual bookshops in China.

Its owner Qian Xiaohua opened this branch of Librairie Avant-Garde in 1999 (there are two other branches in the city, and one in neighbouring Wuxi). The entrance is still Tarmac with rows of books instead of lines of traffic. It's as though you're walking into the mouth of an underground monster. A monster who really, really loves books. When you reach the bottom, finally fully underground, a huge space fans out ahead. The walls are plastered with photographs of bookshops in foreign countries; the counter top has been crafted out of old books, and the manager is always accessible in his open office on the shop floor. And then there are the books: thousands and thousands of them. Surprisingly light for a space with no windows, Librairie Avant-Garde also has a coffee shop, an exhibition space, and room for local businesses to come and sell their products. Every morning, by the time it opens, there's an impatient queue forming outside.

Japan

◆

Jinbōchō, Tokyo

Commonly referred to as Tokyo's Book Town, Jinbōchō is a neighbour-hood of Chiyoda, Toyko, with over seventy bookshops. At the beginning of the twentieth century, after the area had been destroyed by fire, a professor called Shigeo Iwanami decided to rejuvenate it by opening a bookshop. That subsequently became a publishing house, but by then the idea had snowballed, and the Book Town was born. New, second-hand, antiquarian, independent and chain bookshops all nestle together here in a variety of shapes and sizes: where one finishes, the next starts – all slotting together like a game of Tetris. Many simply rent wall space on the outside of buildings to secure their bookshelves to the brickwork, or set out stalls on the pavement.

◆

Buddha Bellies, Tokyo

Three times a week, Ayuko Akiyama holds sushi-making classes in Tokyo's Books on Japan bookshop, which is full of books on Japanese culture. This is her Buddha Bellies Cooking School and people from over thirty different countries have come to take part. They can browse the stock of cook books while they're there. 'I used to teach at a bigger kitchen studio with a lot of equipment,' says Ayuko, 'but I always wanted to do a class that was smaller and more private, in a relaxed environment.

'Then I found this little hidden gem of bookshop with a tiny kitchen, and fell in love with it. For me, a bookshop is still a vivid and alive place that gives us a feeling of warmth. The bookshops here in Tokyo are becoming more of a gathering-space for people, a place of cultural intersection or, as we like to call it, a "third place". Through books, we feel as though the writers' and editors' spirits are still breathing.'

❖

BOOKISH FACT

The first instance of 'book-binding' was performed by the Assyrians in approximately 2,000 BC. They would write their scripts on terracotta tablets and cover them in clay, which would then harden. To prove that no-one had read it before it reached them, the person given the tablet would first have to break the clay, like a wax seal.

Malaysia

◆

Langkawi and Malacca Book Villages

The Langkawi Book Village opened in 1997, selling second-hand books from a house on stilts in the Lubuk Semilang rainforest. The Lubuk Semilang is famous for its rare butterflies, and outside the bookshop you can see Green-Banded Peacocks, Black and White Helens and Golden Birdwings. At Malacca, another book village in Malaysia, there is a café next door to the bookshops that is said to have more monkeys in it than customers!

Thailand

◆

Chatuchak Market, Bangkok

Chatuchak Market in Bangkok is the largest market in Thailand and indeed, with over 15,000 stalls covering more than thirty-five acres and even live animals for sale, it's the largest weekend market in the world. It's pretty crowded, especially on Saturdays with over 200,000 visitors a day, but if it gets too hot a Thai iced-tea maker is never too far away.

Sections 1 and 27 of the market, called the Dream Sections, house a labyrinth of book stalls to get lost in. The books are often piled up from ground, spine-out, up to seven feet high, so if you spy a title in the middle of one of these teetering piles, it might be a little difficult to extract it without pulling the whole shop down – but that's all part of the experience: bookshop Jenga at its best.

★ ★ ★ SOME WONDERFUL THINGS ★ ★ ★

◆ Atta Galatta Bookshop in Bangalore is surrounded by five silver oak trees. It opened a bakery on the ground floor in 2012 selling twenty buns a day, but the nearby tea shops loved them so much that it now turns out 20,000 a day for local businesses.

◆ The Shah M. Book Company in Afghanistan was founded in 1974 and has many outlets in Kabul. Its owner, Shah Muhammad Rais, used to travel to remote parts of the country selling books from a bus.

◆ APODON Bookshop in Xiamen, China, has what they call 'bookshelves in the sky' suspended from the ceiling, with plants along the top of them to symbolise the trees from which books are made.

◆ College Street in Calcutta, India, is known as Boi Para (Colony of Books). Many publishers are based there, and book stalls stretch for half a mile along it.

◆ Shibuya Booksellers in Tokyo separates the books on its shelves not by genre, but by decade, based not on when a book was published, but the period in which it's set. It also publishes its own books, and refers to the bookshop as a bookish bakery: making and selling things in the same space for people to consume.

◆ Diviya Kapur left her job as a lawyer in Delhi to set up her own bookshop, Literati, inside a converted house close to the beach on the coast north of Goa. Sometimes there will be buskers playing in the shop to raise money for local charities. Diviya has a New Book Room and a Second-hand Book Room, and has also opened an Italian café.

◆ The Bookworm in Beijing often has impromptu music evenings that bubble up out of nowhere, normally huddled around the bookshop piano. In some rooms the bookshelves are floor-to-ceiling, and there is an outdoor terrace where they serve cocktails.

◆ Numabookcat was a pop-up bookshop run by NAM Collective in Tokyo in 2011, an art installation shaped like a cat, and constructed out of books! People could come to it for a reading consultation, following which the booksellers would then select six books for them, to be sent on once the exhibition was over.

◆ VVG Something in Taipei, Taiwan, is designed to look like a workshop. A long wooden table runs through the narrow space, and chests of drawers line the walls, with books sticking out of every open drawer.

◆ SAM KEE Bookshop in Hong Kong isn't just a bookshop: it also takes in stray cats, so you'll find cats everywhere, lounging on the shelves and sleeping on top of bookcases.

◆ At the 2014 London Book Fair, Hiroshi Sogo, the Managing Director of Japan's Kinokuniya book chain, revealed that – despite Japan being a very technology-driven country – e-book sales make up as little as 3% of its book market. This isn't just due to publishers' restrictions on e-book availability, he explained, but rather the store that Japan sets by tradition. This doesn't mean, however, that the Kinokuniya bookshops don't make use of technology: customers can give the bookshop their mobile number and, whenever they're within half a mile of the store, it'll text them details of the latest releases in the hope that they'll stop by.

Singapore

♦

BooksActually

BooksActually is one of the most beautiful bookshops I've ever seen, with neat piles of new books everywhere and a bookshop cat sitting by the till. Kenny Leck is the owner:

'Our bookselling days at BooksActually started in October 2005, and we have not really looked back since. The idea was really simple: we loved books, or perhaps the best way to say it: we grew up with too much books. Note the usage of *much* instead of *many*. I have always dreamt of running a business, and with so much books surrounding me, and four years of bookselling under my belt, hey presto, the bookstore was born.

'Fast-forward to the present day: we will be nine years old by the end of 2014, and we have no clue how we manage to pull it off. My accountant is generally very perplexed when he gets round to doing the accounts at the end of the financial year. He says bookstores are closing left and right, up and down, and here we are, still plugging away at it. I tell him, money laundering is the main source of our income...

'But, no, *BooksActually* focuses heavily on what we ourselves, the people running it, like. And it would be LIKE in shout-out-loud caps. What we like to read – you will see it on the bookshelves. This is the most important stocking policy that we have. The music that we listen to daily is also the same music that plays in the bookstore. The magazines that we consume on a monthly basis are the same titles that we sell to our customers. Selfishly, it is a representation of our character, our lives – or a personal fiefdom if this was the medieval age. We have a knack for doing oddly crazy things, too. Our now annual event that we love and hate is the 24-Hour Bookstore. As the name conveys, we literally have the bookstore open for twenty-four hours, and in those long hours we put in place readings or book launches with as many writers as we can. There's also usually a copious amount of caffeine and energy drinks involved.

'We have sort of grown up with our customers, colleagues, and three cats too. We have seen customers who were geeky students channelling their life into this thing called university education, then we saw them dating (must be all that stress from studying), followed by marriage and kids. The kids are being groomed to be future booksellers!

'And of course, we can never avoid the question of e-books killing bookstores – well, at least over here in Singapore. I am the Joker that says, 'Bring it on!' As a tech-driven country, we are well-known to be early adopters when it comes to new tech gadgets. And if suddenly we have three quarters of the population – currently 5.3 million, smaller than the city of London – owning an e-reader, imagine my joy at them actually reading. So, yes, if it helps to increase the readership numbers, let's get them hooked on reading first, and we, these magical creatures called *booksellers*, we will stealthily convert them into print-book lovers, too.'

❖

BOOKISH FACT

The oldest written recipe we know of
is a recipe for beer. It was found on a
Mesopotamian clay tablet dating back
4,000 years, and at the time people
believed the recipe had been given to
them by the god Enki, father of Ninkasi,
the Sumerian goddess of beer.

Indonesia

• A CHAT WITH EMMA CHAPMAN •

Emma Chapman is the author of the novel *How to be a Good Wife*. She lives in Jakarta.

" Since moving to Indonesia I've come to cherish English-language bookshops because they are so hard to come by.

I was ridiculously over-the-moon to discover Aksara, which has a superbly esoteric selection of new and classic books. It's book browsing at its best: you get a sense that each book has been carefully selected. This is why I love independent bookshops: it's like getting a book recommendation from a very bookish friend, one who cares about reading as much as I do. It's the human connection: these books haven't been chosen by an algorithm, but by someone who has actually read them. **"**

South Korea

◆

Pajubookcity

Twenty miles outside of Seoul, you can find a place viewed as a land of promise: this is Pajubookcity. It's a city built on the principles of peace and the enhancement of the human spirit – values imperilled, say its founders, during colonial rule and the Korean War, and threatened more recently by modern Western industrialisation's focus on the self instead of community.

Pajubookcity hope that industry, community and culture will unite around a common passion: books. The city itself is a huge-scale arts project that over the past twenty years has evolved into a custom-built Book Town, with more than 200 publishing companies and forty bookshops. The founders aim to include every aspect of the publishing industry, from writing and editing to production, distribution and bookselling, to create a literary community and regain a 'lost humanity'. There are also art galleries, cafés and a children's theatre, not to mention a typesetting workshop, a children's publisher with a petting zoo, and an art gallery-bookshop dedicated solely to butterflies. The Tan Tan Story House specialises in books for children, as does the Salim Alice House, which is decorated with illustrations from *Alice in Wonderland* and has a train outside that takes visitors on tours of the other bookshops. Ega Old Bookstore is a second-hand bookshop in a tent; the Bomoolsum bookshop is an antiquarian bookshop with exhibitions of books owned by famous authors; the Doosung Paper Gallery has intricate origami displays... It is almost incredible to think that somewhere this amazing actually exists.

❖

BOOKISH FACT

The largest paper encyclopedia ever
made is thought to be the *Yongle
Encyclopedia*, completed in 1407.
It consisted of 11,095 books, containing
some 370 million Chinese characters.

Cambodia

◆

D's Books, Phnom Penh

The first D's Books in Cambodia (there are also branches in Thailand) was opened in 2004 by an American on Street 240 in Phnom Penh behind the Royal Palace, and sells books in a dozen languages. There are now three D's Books in Cambodia, calling themselves 'real bookshops for real book-lovers,' and since 2011, thanks to a rather remarkable woman by the name of Vantha Douk, they have been 100% Cambodian-owned. Her husband John, who also works at the bookshop, explains how Vantha came to run D's Books.

'Like many Khmers in Phnom Penh, Vantha had a poor and often difficult upbringing in rural Cambodia. Her parents did everything they could to afford her a basic education, and she herself studied hard to make it to the city. Once she did, she worked many different jobs to pay her own way through basic English school: handing out leaflets at traffic lights; selling tickets for traditional Khmer Apsara dance shows; waiting tables in a Chinese restaurant; and working as a cashier in a local supermarket. To afford her English classes she would often live on one meal a day.

'By chance, the American who originally opened D's Books in Cambodia was dining in a restaurant where Vantha's aunt worked, and happened to mention to her aunt that he was looking for staff for the new bookshop he was about to open. Her aunt suggested Vantha could work there and, after an interview where she was finally given the chance to use the English she'd studied so hard to learn, Vantha was offered a job. After five months of commitment, hard work and non-stop learning of everything to do with running a bookshop, she was promoted to country manager. Six years later, she achieved the dream she'd had since her very first day working there, and bought all three D's Books in Cambodia. Her success is a testament to her bravery, resourcefulness and intellect. She's an amazing woman.

'Separate to the bookshop, Vantha and I have found sponsors in the UK for some children from her home village to go to English school, and are trying to find more. It's not a charity or an NGO or anything – it's just something we do ourselves because we know how important it is.

'Books are one of the greatest gifts mankind has given itself. They are knowledge, understanding, comfort, imagination; they are the original radio, the original television, the original internet. Real printed paper books have a character, a soul which lives within the feel and smell and sound of the pages, and this could never possibly be re-created on a screen. The various devices available for ebooks may allow a person to carry more books with them, and in many ways that is a good thing, but it in many ways it is a bad thing. It takes away the character of that one book: its magic is lost. Perhaps that is the best way to say it: printed books are magical, and real bookshops keep that magic alive.'

❖

BOOKISH FACT

The smallest book in the world is called *Shiki no Kusabana* (Flowers of the Seasons), and contains the names and illustrations of Japanese flowers. The letters in the book are just 0.01 millimetres wide, impossible to read with the naked eye, and the pages of the book measure just 0.75 millimetres.

Mongolia

◆

Librairie Papillon, Ulaanbaatar

The slogan of Librairie Papillon reads (translated from the original French):

A bookshop depends on its readers, and their intense curiosity.
Come on! Do not hesitate. Sharpen your curiosity, your antennae.
Life is short, and there are many good things to be found in books.
Books are tasty, fulfilling, delicious and rare.

One thing I've learned while researching this book is that we've been declaring the death of the book imminent for such a long time it's laughable (see page xii). But the other thing is that bookshops are full of love stories. Libraire Papillon is the home of one of my favourites, so I've saved it for last.

Sebastien Marneur moved to Mongolia in 1998 to live in the capital, Ulaanbaatar, which literally translates as 'Red Hero'. The city has an odd history: founded in 1639 as a nomadic Buddhist centre, it moved twenty-eight times before finally settling at the foot of the Bogd Khan Uul mountain that separates the steppe zones of the north and south. It's also one of the oldest reserves in the world, having been protected by law since the 1700s.

As much as he loves living in Ulaanbaatar, Sebastien says he found it very difficult to track down French books there, and whenever he returned to France the suitcase-full of books he could bring back would only last him a month (he reads a lot). So he spent his days at work dreaming of opening a bookshop nearby that stocked books in his own language. 'When I'd saved enough money,' says Sebastien, 'I asked my fiancée, who is Mongolian, whether she would like to open up a bookshop with me. Thankfully, she said yes, so I decided to buy her a bookshop as a wedding present. She learned French in six months, and we opened our shop in 2006.'

A bookshop as a wedding gift may just be the best present I've heard of. Sebastien and his wife stock books in Mongolian, French, English, German and many other languages, and they offer free tea and coffee to all of their customers. He likens the atmosphere of his bookshop to the Latin Quarter of Paris: authors from all over the world come to visit, as it's a great place to go on a writing retreat – right in the heart of the Mongolian steppes.

Over the horizon, far beyond where the city runs out, lies the Gobi desert, whose harsh climate sees temperatures reaching +40°C in the summer, and -40°C in the winter, which then rises into the Altai mountains, where the woolly mammoth once roamed. Now the desert and the mountains are home to herders: in the Gobi they breed cashmere goats, raised for their fine hair; in the Altai the Kazakh herders are the only people in the world to hunt with golden eagles, taking eaglets from their nests, rearing them, training them to hunt alongside them as a team, and then, after years of service, releasing them back into the wild. And the most wonderful thing is that, once a year, these herders trek down from the mountains and out of the desert to come into Ulaanbaatar to stock up on supplies. They don't just buy food and clothes: they also buy books. Though their own lives would seem to tell the most amazing stories, they come to Sebastien, this remarkable French man who somehow found himself selling books in the middle of Asia, and ask him to recommend novels for them take back to the desert and the mountains to read. It's an important task: once the herders return to their nomadic communities there isn't another bookshop for hundreds of miles. Those books have to count, and the stories they choose keep them company in elemental conditions. Perhaps a young girl picks out a collection of Gothic fairy tales and reads about Snow White surrounded by the snow. Perhaps her brother picks up Harry Potter and grins at his pet owl, knowing he's gone one better with an eagle by his side.

We've always used stories as a way to pass on our history, as a way to explain things in life that we don't understand. We use them to make us feel connected to everything around us, and to help us escape to another time or place.

Bookshops across the world are full of these stories.

From travelling booksellers and undercover bookshops, to pop-up stalls and community hubs, walking into a good bookshop is like walking into another zone. These places are time machines, spaceships, story-makers, secret-keepers. They are dragon-tamers, dream-catchers, fact-finders and safe places. They are full of infinite possibilities, and tales worth taking home.

Because whether we're in the middle of the desert or in the heart of a city, on the top of a mountain or on an underground train: having good stories to keep us company can mean the whole world.

Life is short, and there are many good things to be found in books. Books are tasty, fulfilling, delicious and rare.

THE BOOKSHOP AT NIGHT

Lights out, security grille
drawn down, the bookshop rests.
It's been a busy day, but now

the love poets can suspend their flirting
and lamenting, the war historians
enjoy a spell, however brief, of truce,

and the whole fretful assembly
of thinkers, arguers, puzzlers and story-tellers
be good, lie still and go to sleep.

Silence and alphabetical order
prevail. Once or twice in the night
some passer-by may peep

yearningly into the dark and fail
to penetrate it. Closed? At three o'clock?
That can't be right!

Christopher Reid

Acknowledgements

So much love and thanks to the many inspiring booksellers, authors and bookshop-lovers I spoke to when writing this book. You are amazing. Thank you for your time and your support.

Thanks to Hugh Barker and Charlie Campbell for championing *The Bookshop Book*, and to Andreas Campomar, Graham Coster, Clive Hebard, Charlie King, Emily Burns and everyone at Constable & Robinson and Little, Brown who have worked hard to support this project. I owe you a lot of cake.

Thanks to Books Are My Bag, and all of the wonderful things they do to help and support bookshops in the UK & Ireland.

Thanks to Tim Godfray, Oren Teicher, Françoise Dubruille, Jessica Faircliff, Lincoln Gould, Joel Becker, Jan Kløvstad, Philip Jones and Nick Scammell for many a bookish chat. Thanks also to those of you who tweeted and emailed me with shout-outs to your favourite bookshops.

Many thanks to Sam and Sandra Barnes for taking me on a road trip to Hay-on-Wye.

And thank you very much indeed to my wonderful family and friends, who resisted the urge to tell me to change the subject when the word 'bookshop' was the only word to come out of my mouth for well over a year. You're very kind people. (Special mention to Miles, who has to listen to my enthusiastic ramblings for longer than anyone else). I would say that I promise to stop talking about bookshops now... but you all know that's never going to happen in a million years. I hope you'll forgive me.

Prose

Page 112: extract from 'An English Room' by Jeanette Winterson reprinted by permission of Peters, Fraser and Dunlop, , on behalf of Jeanette Winterson.

Extract from George Orwell's *Complte Essays* reprinted with permission of Harvill Secker (Random House); extract from *Three Things You Need to Know About Rockets* reprinted with permission of Short Books Ltd; extract from *The Bookshop That Floated Away* reprinted with permission of Constable & Robinson.

Image of the Thames Tunnel Fancy Fair included with permission from Look & Learn / Peter Jackson Collection.

Poetry

'Open for the Strangest Adventures' by Rebecca Perry:

Rebecca Perry graduated from Manchester's Centre for New Writing in 2008 and now lives and works in London. Her pamphlet *little armoured* was published by Seren in 2012 and was a Poetry Book Society Pamphlet Choice. Her first full collection, *Beauty/Beauty*, will be published by Bloodaxe in January 2015.

'The Bookshop at Night' by Christopher Reid:

Christopher Reid has worked as a freelance journalist, a Professor of Creative Writing, a book editor and a poetry editor at Faber and Faber. He is the author of many collections of poetry including *The Song of Lunch*, *A Scattering* (which won the 2009 Costa Book of the Year Award), *Nonsense* and *Katerina Brac*. His most recent volume is *Six Bad Poets*, published by Faber and Faber in 2013.

Index of Bookshops

Index of People